Mammoth Math

Mammoth Math

(with a little help from some elephant shrews)

David Macaulay

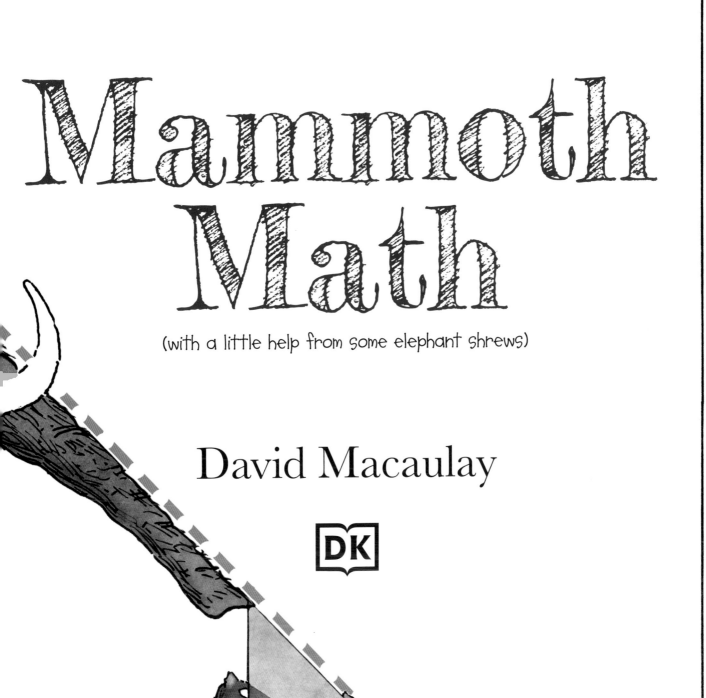

Penguin Random House

Senior Editor Jenny Sich
Senior Art Editor Stefan Podhorodecki
Senior US Editor Megan Douglass
Editors Michelle Crane, Sam Kennedy, Rona Skene
Designer Kit Lane
Senior Jacket Designer Suhita Dharamjit
DTP Designer Rakesh Kumar
Senior Jackets Coordinator Priyanka Sharma-Saddi
Jacket Design Development Manager Sophia MTT
Production Editor Gillian Reid
Production Controller Sian Cheung
Managing Editor Francesca Baines
Managing Art Editor Philip Letsu
Publisher Andrew Macintyre
Art Director Karen Self
Associate Publishing Director Liz Wheeler
Publishing Director Jonathan Metcalf

Text by Rona Skene
Consultant Branka Surla

With thanks to Elizabeth Wise for the index; Hazel Beynon
for proofreading; Carron Brown, Elizabeth Davey, Ashwin Khurana,
and Vicky Richards for additional text and editing

First American Edition, 2022
Published in the United States by DK Publishing
1745 Broadway, 20th Floor, New York, NY 10019

Artwork copyright © 2022 David Macaulay
Text and design copyright © 2022 Dorling Kindersley Limited
DK, a Division of Penguin Random House LLC
23 24 25 26 10 9 8 7 6 5 4 3
008–324983–Jul/2022

A catalog record for this book
is available from the Library of Congress.
ISBN: 978-0-7440-5611-2

DK books are available at special discounts when purchased in bulk
for sales promotions, premiums, fund-raising, or educational use.
For details, contact: DK Publishing Special Markets,
1745 Broadway, 20th Floor, New York, NY 10019
SpecialSales@dk.com

Printed and bound in China

For the curious
www.dk.com

MIX
Paper | Supporting
responsible forestry
FSC™ C018179

This book was made with Forest
Stewardship Council™ certified
paper – one small step in DK's
commitment to a sustainable future.
For more information go to
www.dk.com/our-green-pledge

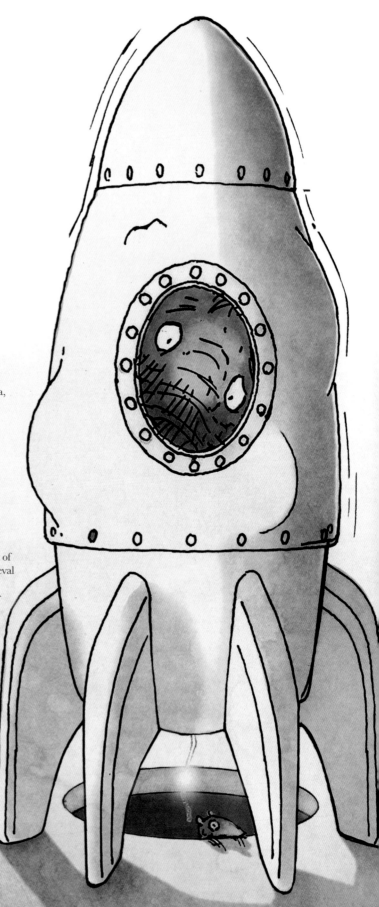

Contents

Count on it!

Keeping count

Being able to count is essential for everything from telling the time to keeping score at a soccer match. Before people had writing or number systems (see pages 12–13), they had to count in their heads (and with whatever they had around to help them). The mammoth and elephant shrews are demonstrating the difficulties of counting their favorite fruit this way, using only bits of their bodies.

Counting in tens
Our number system is based on counting things in groups of 10—probably because counting on fingers and thumbs is so handy.

10

9

8

7

6

5

4

3

2

1

Using fingers and toes
Fingers (or mammoth toes) are convenient things to help keep track of numbers less than 10. The shrew works his way from toe to toe, touching one for each apple, counting 8 in total.

Too many apples
With this many objects to keep track of, counting on body parts can be tricky.

Body work
You could assign numbers to as many body parts as you want—as long as you can remember what they all stand for.

You can count on a mammoth
If you have no words or symbols for numbers, bodies can be useful for helping to count. Touching fingers or other bits of the body as you count helps you keep track. You can also hold fingers up to tell someone else how many of something you have.

Eight toes, eight apples
For each apple, the shrew taps a mammoth toe.

Counting beyond 10
If you need to count numbers larger than 10, you could add more body parts. The mammoth has tried to count a lot of apples like this and got into a muddle. Maybe tallying (see pages 10–11) would work better?

Counting without counting
Sometimes we know how many things there are without having to count them. With a small group of things, we can often tell how many there are just by looking. This amazing skill we all have is called subitizing. Most of us can easily do this with groups of up to five. And we use it for larger numbers, by seeing smaller groups and adding them together. Can you see how many pies there are here, without counting them?

Tallying to keep count

Counting on fingers, toes, or other body parts is fine, as long you've got a good enough memory to keep track of what you've counted. Keeping a written record is often a much better idea. Tallying is making a stroke or scratch mark for each thing you're counting, such as every time the sun rises or how many mammoths there are in the herd.

Tally ho!

When you're counting a herd in a hurry, the simplest way is to make one straight line for each mammoth. But all those marks soon add up and become hard to keep track of—imagine how long it would take to count all the marks to get to 100! It's quicker to make groups of marks, and count the groups instead.

Making your mark
Each vertical line represents one mammoth. The elephant shrew draws a line for each mammoth that goes past.

Making tallying easier
Tally marks are still useful today, especially to count things that are moving quickly—like traffic for example. Grouping the marks means you can count groups instead of individual marks, which is quicker and easier. There are different ways of tallying—all these examples show groups of five marks. The first makes a simple "gate" shape. The second builds into a Chinese character. The last method makes a square with a diagonal line through it.

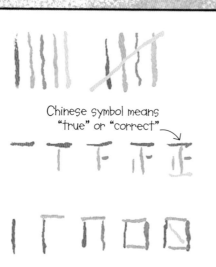

Chinese symbol means "true" or "correct"

Straight gates
To make it easier to keep
track, every fifth tally mark is a
diagonal line drawn over the
first four marks. These sets of
marks are called five–bar gates.

Temporary tallies
If you count a lot of items, you will
end up with a lot of marks! To find
your total, count how many lots of
5 you have. But if your tally gets
trampled then it is back to
square one.

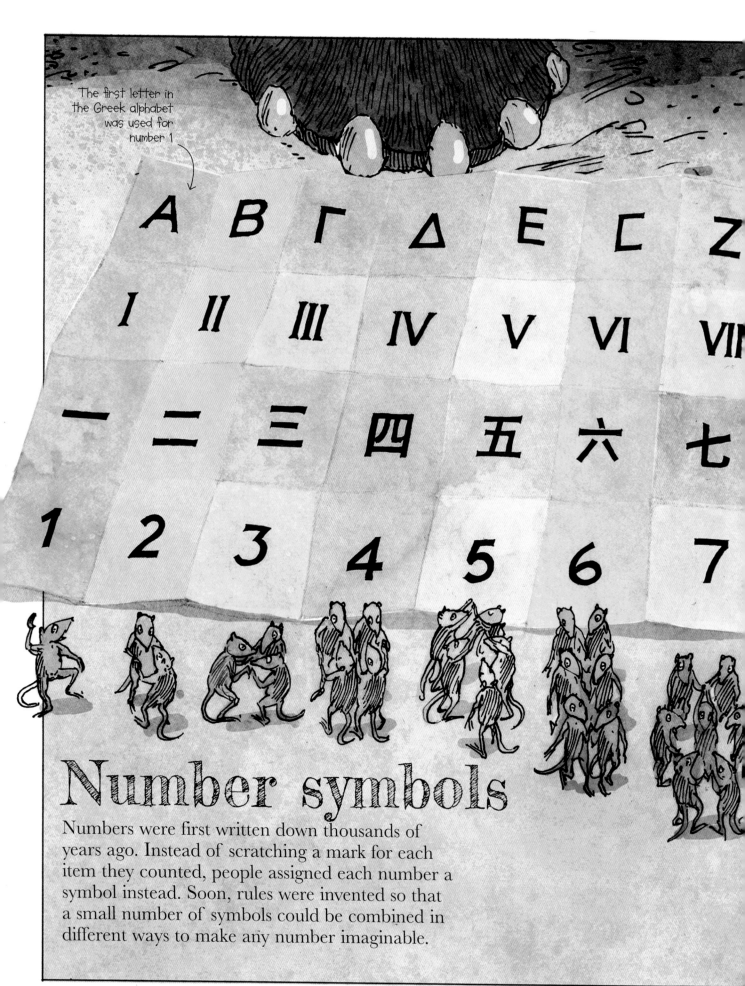

The first letter in the Greek alphabet was used for number 1

Number symbols

Numbers were first written down thousands of years ago. Instead of scratching a mark for each item they counted, people assigned each number a symbol instead. Soon, rules were invented so that a small number of symbols could be combined in different ways to make any number imaginable.

Number systems

The elephant shrews are comparing the numbers 1 to 10 in different number systems. Many systems have been invented throughout history, each with its own set of rules for combining symbols to make the number you want to show. The number system we use today was invented in India more than 1,000 years ago.

Ancient Greek
In this system the letters of the alphabet were recycled to stand for numbers, too.

Ancient Roman
This system also used letters, putting them together in different ways to make numbers.

Ancient Chinese
Each number from 1 to 10 had its own symbol, and there were different symbols for multiples of 10: 100; 1,000; and so on.

Hindu–Arabic
The world's most common system is different from those that came before it because it has the symbol zero (0). See pages 16–17 to find out why zero is a hero!

Never-ending numbers
The Hindu-Arabic system uses the digits 1–9 and the symbol 0. Each digit represents a given amount, but these digits can also be used in combination to create an infinite amount of other numbers (see pages 14–15).

Place value

Numbers are made up of symbols called digits: our number system uses the digits 0–9. But the value of these digits can change. For example, in the number 20, the "2" stands for a different amount than it does in the number 200. The amount a digit is worth depends on its position in the number. This is called place value.

Counting in 10s

It's full steam ahead at the apple-packing plant. Mammoths and elephant shrews are sorting the apples into sets of 10. Each time a set of 10 fills up, it moves a place to the left. Our counting system works like this, too—we call it the base-10, or decimal, system. So far, 1,453 apples have been packed.

Hundreds
Each tray contains 10 tubes of 10 apples—which makes 100 apples per tray.

Thousands
A pallet holds 10 trays, and each tray contains 100 apples. So there are 1,000 apples on this pallet.

One thousand
When there are 10 full trays in the "100s" stack, they move to the left, into the "1,000s." There is one full pallet at this station, which means that there are 1,000 apples.

Four hundreds
When the tens trays are full, they move into the hundreds stack. There are 4 full trays here, so that's 4 lots of 100, or 400 apples.

Hold that space!

For the place value system to work, there needs to be a way of showing when a place is empty. This is the special job that zero does (see pages 16–17). In the example below, there are no hundreds in the hundreds column. But without zero to hold the place, we'd be left with 176—a completely different number.

Thousands	Hundreds	Tens	Ones
1	0	7	6

Tens
There is room for 10 tubes of 10 apples in a tray. When it fills up, the tray moves left into the 100s stack.

Ones
Once there are 10 apples in the tube, it will move to the left into the tens tray.

Five tens
Another mammoth lines up the full tubes in a tray. There are 5 full tubes in the tray so far, which means there are 5 lots of ten, or 50 apples, in the tray.

Three ones
The mammoth puts single apples into a tube. There are 3 apples in the tube, so the elephant shrew writes a "3" on the sign.

Zero

Everyone knows that "zero" means "nothing." But zero isn't just nothing, it's a math hero with some very important functions. For thousands of years, people did math without using zero—it was not even considered a number in its own right. Today, it's hard to imagine life without it—things would be very confusing indeed!

Hardworking number

Modern math could not exist without zero— it is essential to the method of place value that underpins our number system. But everyday life would be much more difficult without zero, too. We need it when we tell the time, take a temperature, or keep score in a sports contest. Here, the mammoths show some of the most useful things that zero does.

Nothing at all
Zero often means "nothing" or "empty," but you can't count to zero—you can't count something that's not there. Look at the pictures above. You wouldn't say there were zero mammoths in the bottom picture, unless you'd already seen the picture above.

Calculating with zero

Zero is the only number on the number line that's neither positive or negative, and neither odd nor even. It is a number that has puzzled mathematicians because it doesn't work quite the same way as other numbers do. For example, you can add, subtract, and multiply with zero, but you can't divide by zero.

$$8 + 0 = 8$$

$$8 - 0 = 8$$

$$8 \times 0 = 0$$

$$8 \div 0 = ????$$

There is no answer that would make sense here

Digital language
Computers communicate in zeros. Binary code is the system we use to give computers their orders: instructions are translated into sequences made up only of 1s and 0s.

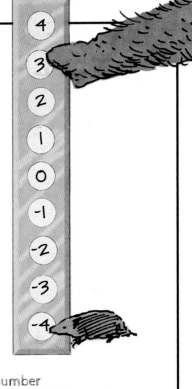

Keeping score

Without zero, it would be harder to keep track in a soccer match—the "zero" symbol tells us that the blue team hasn't scored a goal.

A real number

Zero is a number with its own place on the number line, where it's the dividing point between negative and positive numbers. In an elevator, "0" can be used for the ground floor—positive numbers are floors above ground and negative numbers are below ground level.

Without zero, we couldn't tell the difference between 21 and 201!

Taking measurements

When we measure things, zero is a set amount with its own value. The thermometer says 0°, but that doesn't mean there's no temperature—0° describes a value on the scale.

Showing place value

Zero is essential to our number system. The value of each digit in a number depends on its position (see pages 14–15). Zero "holds the place" of a value when there is no other digit to go in that position.

Negative numbers

Any number that is greater than zero is a positive number. If you count down from zero, you go into negative numbers. These are numbers that are less than zero. They are shown with a negative sign (-) in front of them.

A door on every floor

The elephant shrews have built themselves a multilevel housing complex. Each burrow is on a separate floor. Those above ground level (which is marked with a "0") are given positive burrow numbers. The ones beneath ground level have negative numbers on their doormats.

Zero in the middle
Zero (0) is not positive or negative. It's the number that separates positive and negative numbers.

Counting down
Negative numbers count backward from zero. The farther away from zero it is, the lower the number will be.

Lower and lower
−4 is less than −3, because it is farther away from 0.

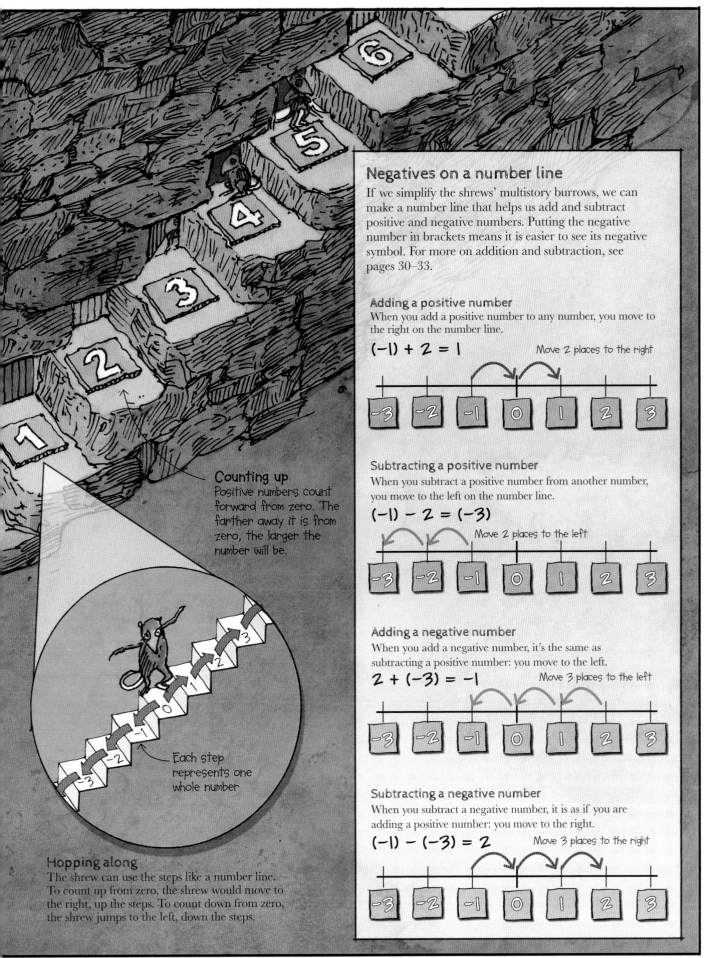

Counting up

Positive numbers count forward from zero. The farther away it is from zero, the larger the number will be.

Each step represents one whole number

Hopping along

The shrew can use the steps like a number line. To count up from zero, the shrew would move to the right, up the steps. To count down from zero, the shrew jumps to the left, down the steps.

Negatives on a number line

If we simplify the shrews' multistory burrows, we can make a number line that helps us add and subtract positive and negative numbers. Putting the negative number in brackets means it is easier to see its negative symbol. For more on addition and subtraction, see pages 30–33.

Adding a positive number

When you add a positive number to any number, you move to the right on the number line.

$$(-1) + 2 = 1$$

Move 2 places to the right

Subtracting a positive number

When you subtract a positive number from another number, you move to the left on the number line.

$$(-1) - 2 = (-3)$$

Move 2 places to the left

Adding a negative number

When you add a negative number, it's the same as subtracting a positive number: you move to the left.

$$2 + (-3) = -1$$

Move 3 places to the left

Subtracting a negative number

When you subtract a negative number, it is as if you are adding a positive number: you move to the right.

$$(-1) - (-3) = 2$$

Move 3 places to the right

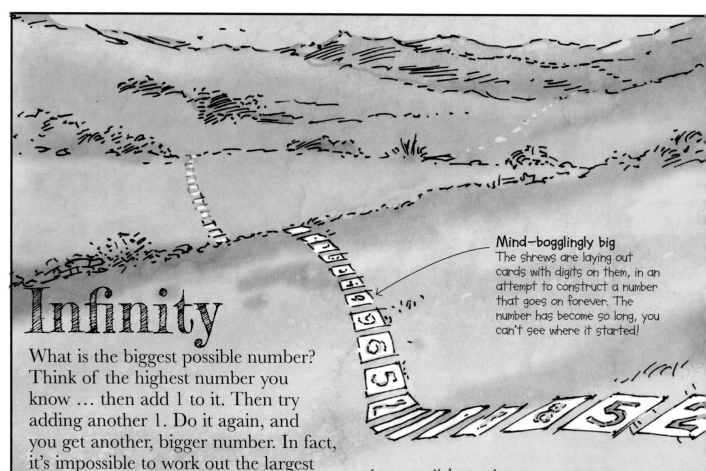

Infinity

What is the biggest possible number? Think of the highest number you know … then add 1 to it. Then try adding another 1. Do it again, and you get another, bigger number. In fact, it's impossible to work out the largest number, because there's no limit to how big (or small) a number can be. In math, we say that numbers are infinite.

Mind–bogglingly big

The shrews are laying out cards with digits on them, in an attempt to construct a number that goes on forever. The number has become so long, you can't see where it started!

Impossible task

These determined elephant shrews have set out, with the mammoths' help, to create the world's longest number. But no matter how long they keep at it, they'll never succeed, because numbers are infinite. The word "infinite" doesn't actually mean "really big"—it means "never-ending"!

Never-ending symbol

This is the symbol for infinity: it looks like a figure 8 on its side. It's the perfect symbol to use because, like infinity itself, it's got no beginning or end.

Calculations involving infinity don't have the results you might expect. Subtract 1 from infinity and you've still got infinity! This is because infinity isn't actually a number, it's an idea.

$$\infty - 1 = \infty$$
$$50\% \text{ of } \infty = \infty$$

Infinite supply
The shrews are going to need an infinite number of cards—and an infinite amount of energy!

To infinity ... and beyond!
It's not just numbers that are infinite—time and space might be, too. An infinite amount of time stretching back and forward forever is called eternity. The universe contains everything that exists—every galaxy, star, or planet that there ever was or will be. Some scientists think that the universe is infinite, while others think it has an outer limit and therefore is finite. We'll probably never know for sure.

On and on
The shrews keep adding digits but they will always be able to add one more.

Number
know-how

Ordering numbers

If you want to put numbers in order, you have to compare them first. Comparing one number with another tells you whether it is greater than, less than, or equal to the other. To crown the winner of this hotly contested talent show, the judges must carefully compare the scores.

Votes are in!

The phone-in votes have been counted and the results are in. By comparing the numbers, the scores can be listed from highest to lowest on the scoreboard and the performer with the most votes will be the winner.

Trailing behind
11,256 is less than 27,002 (or, using symbols, 11,256 < 27,002).

11,256

In a twirl
This whirling wonder doesn't seem to have impressed the audience.

Worthy winner?
The elephant shrew has more votes than the acts in second place: 27,002 > 22,405.

27,002

Strong shrew
This small but mighty contender has made a big impression, sweeping to victory!

Symbols

We can use symbols to show when numbers are bigger or smaller than each other. The wide end of the symbol always points to the bigger number. Two parallel lines mean two numbers are equal to each other.

Less than
This symbol means "less than." 10 < 12 means "10 is less than 12."

Greater than
This symbol means "greater than." 12 > 10 means "12 is greater than 10."

Equal to
Numbers separated by this symbol have the same value.

Most significant digit → 27,002

Second significant digit → 22,405

22,405

11,256

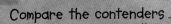
Compare the contenders
To put the numbers in order we compare their most significant digit—the one with the highest place value. If these are the same, carry on comparing digits from left to right.

22,405

Spinning spectacle
Some shrews liked this act, but not enough to propel the plate spinner to victory.

Tied for second place
The magician and the plate spinner received exactly the same number of votes. We say these numbers are equal (22,405 = 22,405).

22,405

Magic mammoth
The magician's many magic tricks have sadly not brought success.

Estimating

Math is often about getting the right answer, but sometimes it can be useful to make an estimate, or sensible guess, especially when very big numbers are involved or you have a lot of objects that would take far too long to count. Estimates can also help when checking calculations, to make sure the answer you get is in a similar range to your rough guess.

Tough crowd
There are far too many excitable elephant shrews to count easily.

Count one square
Pick one square in your grid and count the number of shrews it contains.

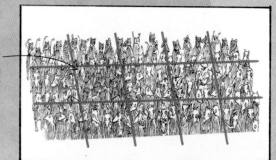

Sea of shrews

It's tricky to count a crowd of elephant shrews who are constantly jumping in and out of their seats. Luckily, there are ways to make a quick, sensible guess. The actual number of shrews is 110, so let's see how close we can get by using two different methods.

Using a grid

You can estimate the total by dividing the group into roughly equal imaginary squares. There are 8 shrews in the highlighted square. Multiply 8 by 15 (the number of squares), and you get a guess of 120 shrews.

Using rows

Another method is to count the shrews in one row, then multiply by the number of rows. There are 20 shrews in the front row and 5 rather uneven rows. So by this method, the estimate is 100 shrews.

Savvy shopping

When you're buying things, estimation is a quick way to see if you're keeping to your budget. With these three items, you can make the calculation easier by saying that the popcorn costs about $2, the drink is about $1, and the ice cream is about $1.50. So your estimate of the total cost of this snack-fest is $4.50. The actual cost would be $4.53, so that's a pretty useful guess.

$2.19

$0.89

$1.45

Rounding

Rounding a number is changing it to one close in value, often one that is easier to calculate with. Rounding to the nearest 10 makes it much easier to add, subtract, or multiply numbers quickly in your head, and is particularly useful when making a rough estimate (see pages 26–27).

Up or down?

How do you know whether to round up or down? Use the roller coaster to remember the rounding rule! For digits less than 5, you round down. For 5 and above, round up.

Rounding down

If the last digit of your number is 4 or below, you round down. For example, 73 rounds down to 70, not up to 80. The elephant shrews on this part of the roller coaster are headed back down the hill.

Which way?

This muddled mammoth wants to round 65 to the nearest ten. Should it be rounded up to 70 or down to 60? The rule says that 5 rounds up, so 65 rounds up to 70.

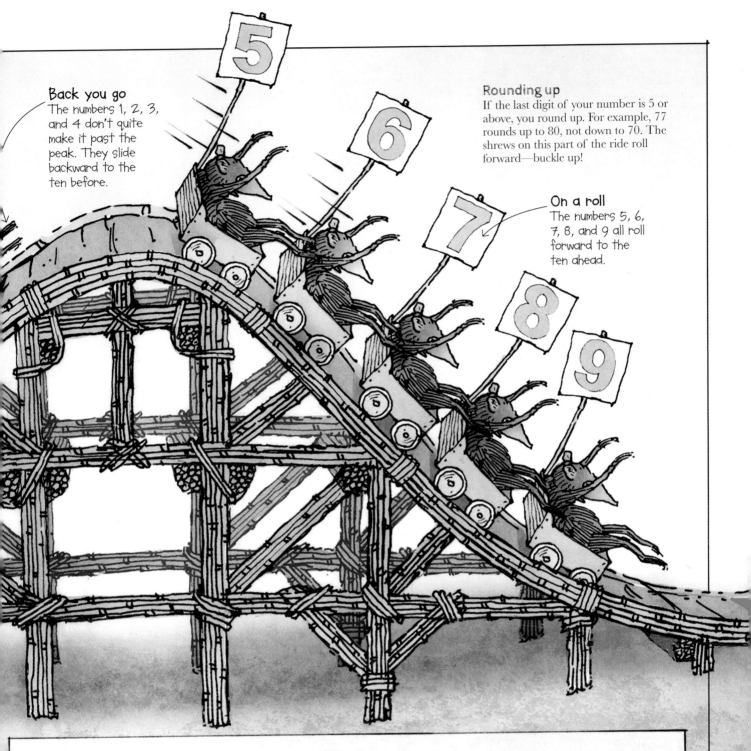

Back you go
The numbers 1, 2, 3, and 4 don't quite make it past the peak. They slide backward to the ten before.

Rounding up
If the last digit of your number is 5 or above, you round up. For example, 77 rounds up to 80, not down to 70. The shrews on this part of the ride roll forward—buckle up!

On a roll
The numbers 5, 6, 7, 8, and 9 all roll forward to the ten ahead.

Rounding hundreds
If you want to round to the nearest hundred, the same rounding rule applies. When rounding to the nearest ten, you look at the ones digit. When rounding to the nearest hundred, look at the tens digit instead. You can use the rounding rule to round fractions and decimals, too.

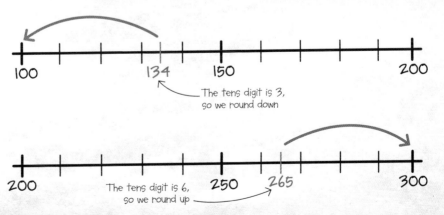

100   134   150   200

The tens digit is 3, so we round down

200   250   265   300

The tens digit is 6, so we round up

Addition

Putting two or more quantities together to make a bigger quantity is called addition. Whether you are adding very big numbers or small, simple amounts, there are two main ways to think about addition, as the mammoths are discovering on their day out at the fair.

Fair fun

Roll up, roll up—the fair has come to town! At the coconut shy, the elephant shrews are putting the finishing touches to their stall, adding the final few coconuts onto stands. Elsewhere, two mammoths have won some colorful balloons, but how many do they have in total?

Counting on

One way of thinking about addition is called counting on. You start with one number, then count forward the number of places you need to add. To fill their empty coconut stands, the shrews start from the number already on stands—6—and add 3 more. This is known as counting on.

Larger number
Starting with the largest number and counting on from that is quicker than starting from a smaller one.

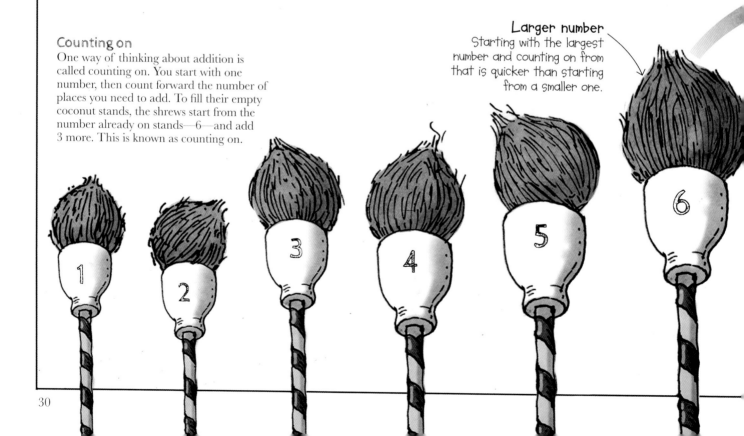

Counting all

The other way of thinking about addition is to put the amounts together into one group, and then count them all. Putting the purple and yellow helium balloons together makes one group for the mammoth to count.

Up and away!

This airborne mammoth has one group of 9 balloons.

Writing down addition

Often, adding numbers together is a mental skill—we can work out the answer in our heads by looking at the numbers. But sometimes we need a written method to find the total. We write addition number sentences using the "+" or "add" symbol to show when numbers are being added together. Adding works in any order. If we swap the numbers around, the total will still be the same. For example, 3 + 6 and 6 + 3 both equal 9.

$$6 + 3 = 9$$

This symbol means add, or plus

This symbol means equivalent to, or equals

The result is called the sum

+1

+1

1

The result

Filling up 3 more stands means the shrews have 9 coconuts in total.

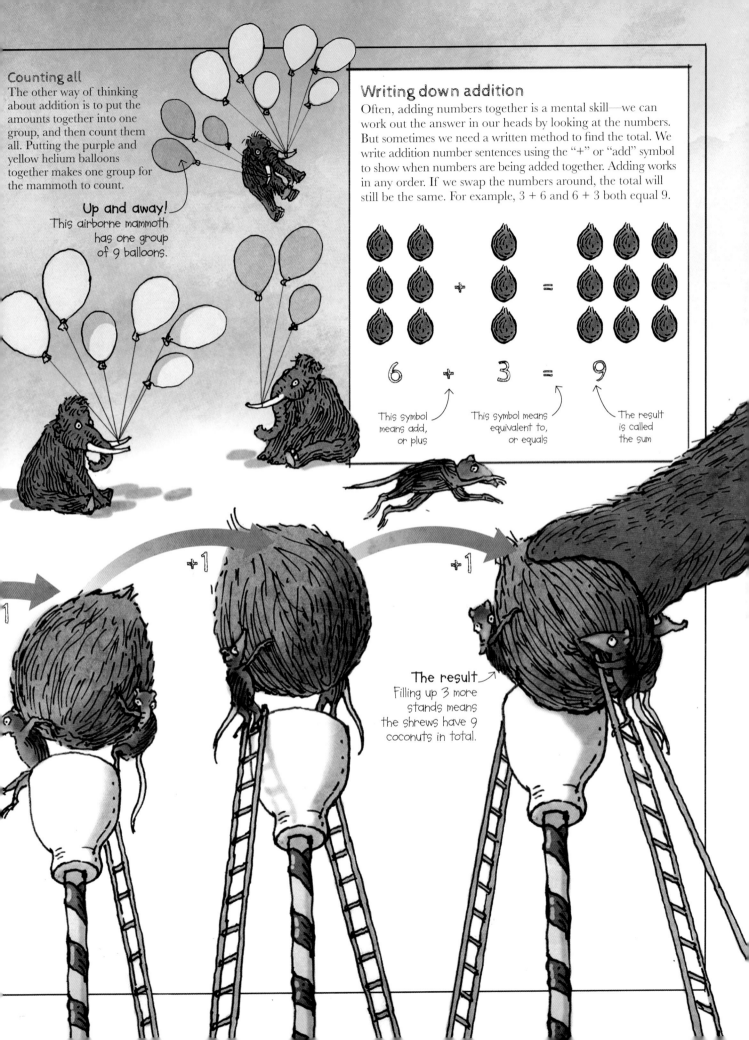

Line them up
It's easier to count back when numbers are arranged in a line.

Finding the difference
The mammoth started off with 9 rocks, and has now thrown 3 of them. There are 6 rocks left in the box—so the difference between 9 and 3 is 6.

Subtraction

Taking one number away from another to find out what's left is called subtraction. It is the inverse, or the opposite, of addition. You can think about subtraction as counting back, or as finding the difference between two numbers.

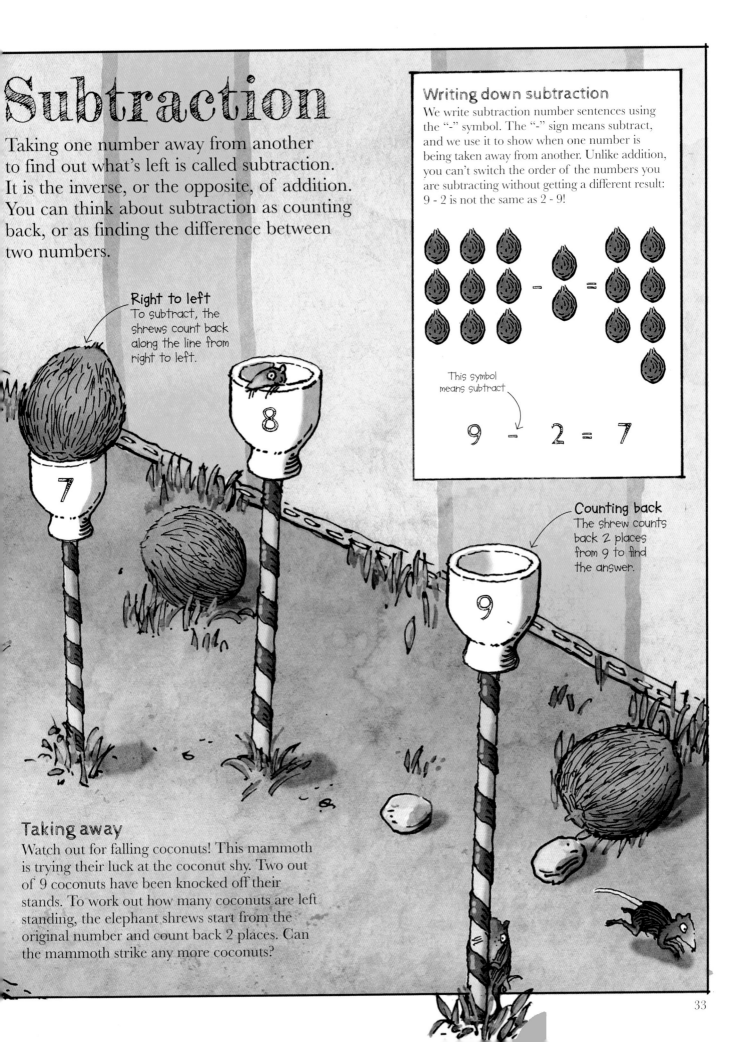

Right to left
To subtract, the shrews count back along the line from right to left.

Writing down subtraction
We write subtraction number sentences using the "-" symbol. The "-" sign means subtract, and we use it to show when one number is being taken away from another. Unlike addition, you can't switch the order of the numbers you are subtracting without getting a different result: 9 - 2 is not the same as 2 - 9!

This symbol means subtract

$$9 - 2 = 7$$

Counting back
The shrew counts back 2 places from 9 to find the answer.

Taking away
Watch out for falling coconuts! This mammoth is trying their luck at the coconut shy. Two out of 9 coconuts have been knocked off their stands. To work out how many coconuts are left standing, the elephant shrews start from the original number and count back 2 places. Can the mammoth strike any more coconuts?

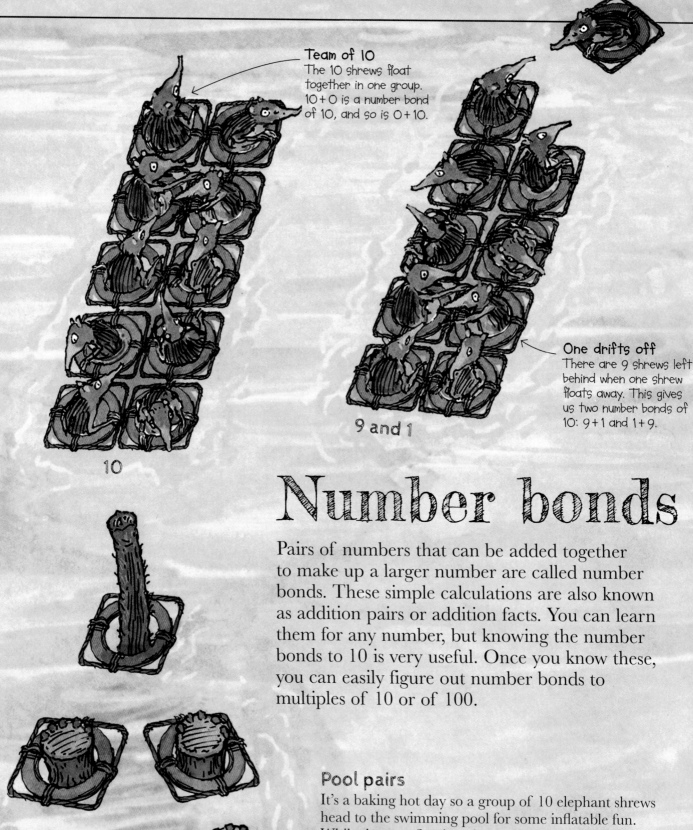

Team of 10
The 10 shrews float together in one group. 10 + 0 is a number bond of 10, and so is 0 + 10.

10

9 and 1

One drifts off
There are 9 shrews left behind when one shrew floats away. This gives us two number bonds of 10: 9 + 1 and 1 + 9.

Number bonds

Pairs of numbers that can be added together to make up a larger number are called number bonds. These simple calculations are also known as addition pairs or addition facts. You can learn them for any number, but knowing the number bonds to 10 is very useful. Once you know these, you can easily figure out number bonds to multiples of 10 or of 100.

Pool pairs

It's a baking hot day so a group of 10 elephant shrews head to the swimming pool for some inflatable fun. While they are floating along together, one of the shrews drifts away from the group. The shrews have formed an addition pair, or number bond, of 10. They decide to rearrange themselves into two groups in as many different ways as they can, making all the number bonds to 10.

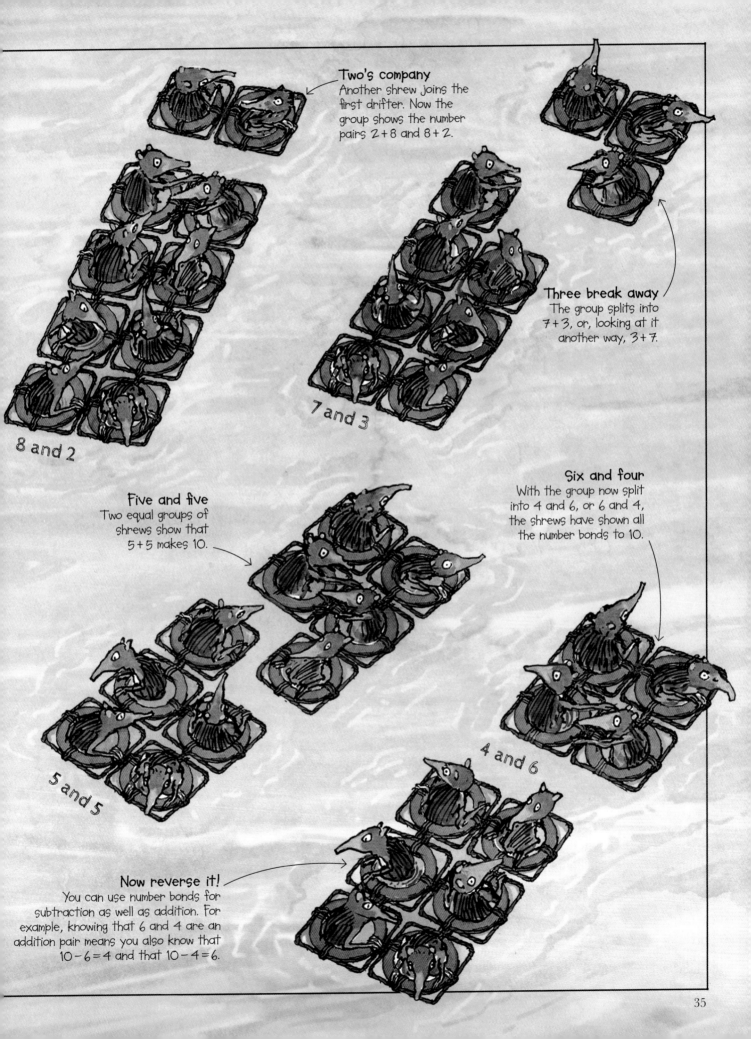

Two's company
Another shrew joins the first drifter. Now the group shows the number pairs 2 + 8 and 8 + 2.

Three break away
The group splits into 7 + 3, or, looking at it another way, 3 + 7.

8 and 2

7 and 3

Six and four
With the group now split into 4 and 6, or 6 and 4, the shrews have shown all the number bonds to 10.

Five and five
Two equal groups of shrews show that 5 + 5 makes 10.

5 and 5

4 and 6

Now reverse it!
You can use number bonds for subtraction as well as addition. For example, knowing that 6 and 4 are an addition pair means you also know that 10 − 6 = 4 and that 10 − 4 = 6.

Multiplication

Multiplying is really just a quick way of adding the same number over and over. When we write "5 x 3," it means exactly the same as "5 + 5 + 5," or "three groups of 5." The cross symbol (x) means "multiply by," or "times."

Product
The result of a multiplication is called the product.

$$5 \times 3 = 15$$

Mammoth multiplying

During their artistic swimming routine, a team of 15 mammoths organize themselves into smaller groups—first of five, then of three. This shows perfectly the rule of multiplying—that it doesn't matter which way around you multiply two numbers, the answer will be the same.

Three groups of five

This formation (in math it's called an array) has 3 rows, each with 5 mammoths. The numbers 3 and 5 form a pair of numbers that, when multiplied together, always make 15.

5 in a row
Each row has 5 mammoths.

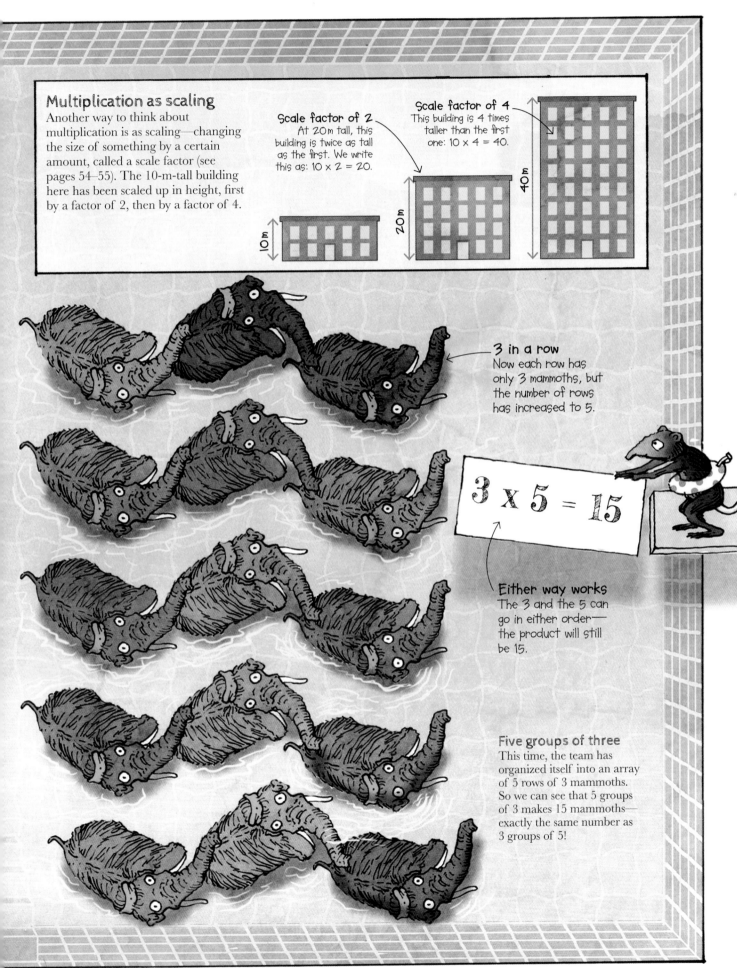

Multiplication as scaling

Another way to think about multiplication is as scaling—changing the size of something by a certain amount, called a scale factor (see pages 54–55). The 10-m-tall building here has been scaled up in height, first by a factor of 2, then by a factor of 4.

Scale factor of 2
At 20m tall, this building is twice as tall as the first. We write this as: 10 × 2 = 20.

Scale factor of 4
This building is 4 times taller than the first one: 10 × 4 = 40.

10m

20m

40m

3 in a row
Now each row has only 3 mammoths, but the number of rows has increased to 5.

$3 \times 5 = 15$

Either way works
The 3 and the 5 can go in either order— the product will still be 15.

Five groups of three
This time, the team has organized itself into an array of 5 rows of 3 mammoths. So we can see that 5 groups of 3 makes 15 mammoths— exactly the same number as 3 groups of 5!

Division

Division is the math term to describe splitting or sharing a number or amount into smaller equal amounts. It's also a way of finding out how many times one number fits into another. Division is the opposite, or inverse, of multiplication.

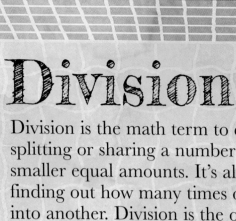

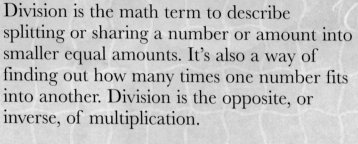

$$15 \div 3 = 5$$

Making groups of 3

When the 15 swimming mammoths split into groups of 3, they form 5 groups. If they divided into groups of 5, there would be 3 groups. The numbers 5 and 3 make a pair: if you divide 15 by one of them, the result is the other number.

How many times?
The inverse of this operation is 5 x 3 = 15.

Groups of 3
The 15 team members divide exactly into 5 groups of 3, with no mammoths left over.

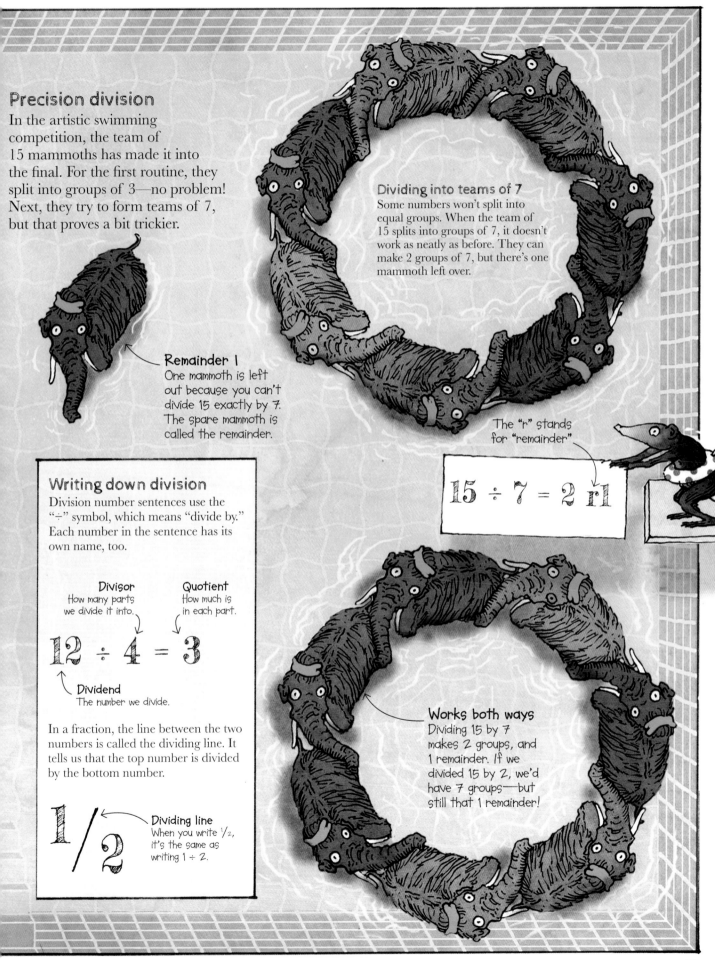

Precision division

In the artistic swimming competition, the team of 15 mammoths has made it into the final. For the first routine, they split into groups of 3—no problem! Next, they try to form teams of 7, but that proves a bit trickier.

Remainder 1
One mammoth is left out because you can't divide 15 exactly by 7. The spare mammoth is called the remainder.

Dividing into teams of 7
Some numbers won't split into equal groups. When the team of 15 splits into groups of 7, it doesn't work as neatly as before. They can make 2 groups of 7, but there's one mammoth left over.

The "r" stands for "remainder"

$$15 \div 7 = 2 \text{ r1}$$

Writing down division
Division number sentences use the "÷" symbol, which means "divide by." Each number in the sentence has its own name, too.

Divisor
How many parts we divide it into.

Quotient
How much is in each part.

$$12 \div 4 = 3$$

Dividend
The number we divide.

In a fraction, the line between the two numbers is called the dividing line. It tells us that the top number is divided by the bottom number.

$$1/2$$

Dividing line
When you write ½, it's the same as writing 1 ÷ 2.

Works both ways
Dividing 15 by 7 makes 2 groups, and 1 remainder. If we divided 15 by 2, we'd have 7 groups—but still that 1 remainder!

Factors

When you break a number up into equal parts you are splitting it into its factors. A factor is a number that divides exactly into a larger number without leaving a remainder. Every number has at least two factors because a number can be divided by 1 and by itself. Factors always come in pairs, as this energetic team of mammoths are finding out.

1 group of 12

1. Working as one
The 12 mammoths need to stay together in one single group to lift this heavy bus. There is one team of 12 mammoths—that means both 1 and 12 are factors of 12.

Fun factor
This gang of 12 tireless mammoths are taking part in different activities. For each popular pastime, the group has to divide differently. By splitting into equal groups, the mammoths are finding out all the factors of 12: 1, 2, 3, 4, 6, and 12.

Factor trees
Once you have found a number's factors, you can break those factors down again into each of their factors. If you carry on, you'll eventually reach a prime number (see pages 60–61) that can only be divided by 1 and itself. These are called prime factors. To find prime factors, you can make a factor tree. There are often lots of ways to make a factor tree, but you'll always find the same prime factors.

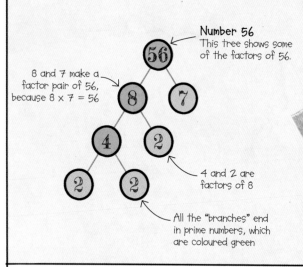

Number 56
This tree shows some of the factors of 56.

8 and 7 make a factor pair of 56, because 8 × 7 = 56

4 and 2 are factors of 8

All the "branches" end in prime numbers, which are coloured green

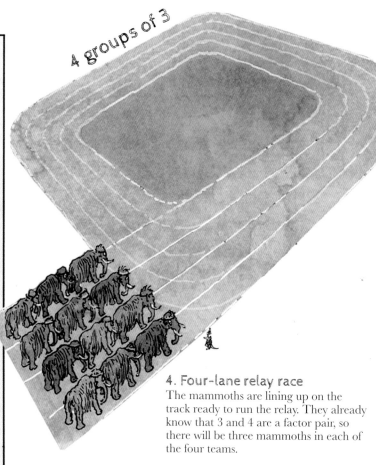

4 groups of 3

4. Four-lane relay race
The mammoths are lining up on the track ready to run the relay. They already know that 3 and 4 are a factor pair, so there will be three mammoths in each of the four teams.

2 groups of 6

2. Two teams
For a game of volleyball, the mammoths need two equal-size teams. When they split in half each team has six mammoths, so both 2 and 6 must also be factors of 12.

3 groups of 4

3. Three-way charades
Now the mammoths are playing charades. The mammoth in the middle is performing for her teammates. There are three teams of four for this game, so 3 and 4 are both factors of 12.

6 groups of 2

5. Six pairs
Some games only need two players. The mammoth gang split into six groups of two for these head-to-head contests: 2 and 6 are factors of 12.

12 groups of 1

6. Freestyle!
The mammoths round off their day of fun each doing their own favorite activity. There are 12 groups of one mammoth each giving it their all, so 12 and 1 are factors of 12.

1 mammoth = ?

Balancing act

An equation has to balance: both sides must have the same value so that the statement is correct. The mammoth's see-saw is like an equation. The mammoth sits on one side and weights are added to the other. The see-saw will only balance when there is exactly the same amount of weight on both sides.

Equations

An equation is a kind of number sentence (math statement) that always contains an equals sign (=). When you see this sign you know that whatever is on one side of it has exactly the same value as what is on the other side. You can write equations with numbers or use symbols to stand for numbers. This is called algebra.

1 mammoth

Too light
With a 1–ton weight on this side, the see–saw isn't level—one side is carrying much more weight than the other.

Unbalanced
There is a mammoth on one side of the see-saw and a 1-ton weight on the other. The see-saw is unbalanced, so that means that 1 mammoth doesn't equal 1 ton.

Balanced
With four weights stacked on the side opposite the mammoth, the see-saw now balances. So now that we know that 1 mammoth is equal to 4 tons, we can write an equation:
1 mammoth = 4 tons.

Just right
Once 4 tons are added, the see-saw is level—the two sides are balanced.

Equals sign
When you see this sign, you know that the two sides must be balanced.

= **4 tons**

Balancing equations
In any equation, the two sides must stay equal. You can use this fact to find out values you don't yet know. In math, we often use a symbol, such as a letter, for the we don't know—this makes the unknown value easier to work with.

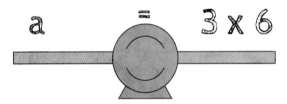

Number equation
In this equation, we know all the values. On one side of the equals sign is 7 + 4, and on the other is 11. The equation balances because the sum of 7 and 4 is 11.

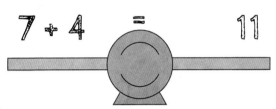

Equation with letters
This equation has a value we don't know yet. The letter "a" stands for the unknown amount—also known as a variable. To find what "a" stands for, we just have to multiply 3 x 6. The unknown quantity must be 18, so that the equation balances.

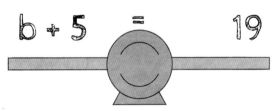

Rearranging equations
To find out the unknown value here, we could rearrange the equation. As long as we do the same thing to each side, the equation will still balance. In this example, we can subtract 5 from each side to give b = 19 - 5, and solve this with simple subtraction to find b = 14.

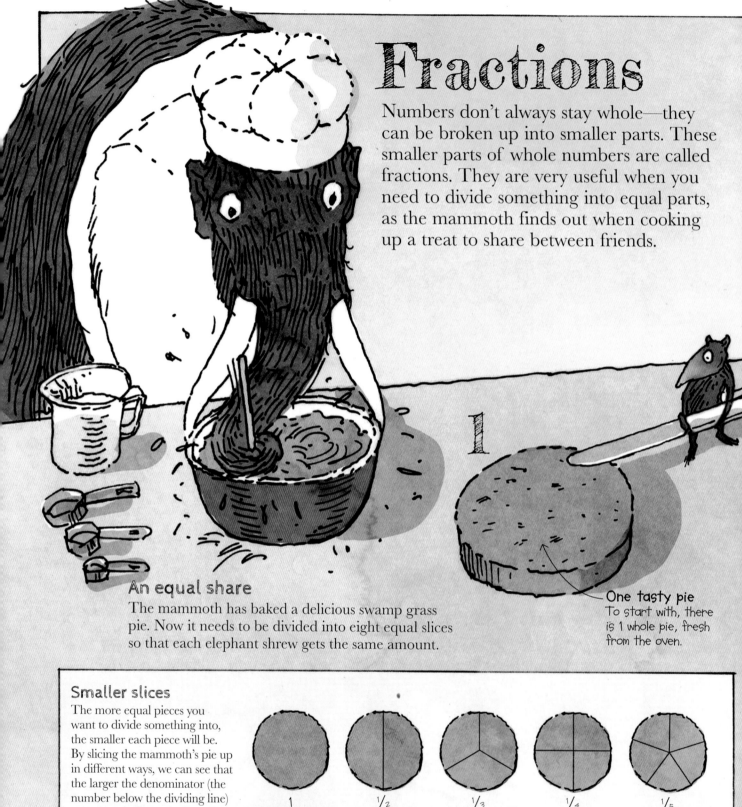

Fractions

Numbers don't always stay whole—they can be broken up into smaller parts. These smaller parts of whole numbers are called fractions. They are very useful when you need to divide something into equal parts, as the mammoth finds out when cooking up a treat to share between friends.

An equal share

The mammoth has baked a delicious swamp grass pie. Now it needs to be divided into eight equal slices so that each elephant shrew gets the same amount.

One tasty pie

To start with, there is 1 whole pie, fresh from the oven.

Smaller slices

The more equal pieces you want to divide something into, the smaller each piece will be. By slicing the mammoth's pie up in different ways, we can see that the larger the denominator (the number below the dividing line) gets, the smaller each slice of the pie becomes.

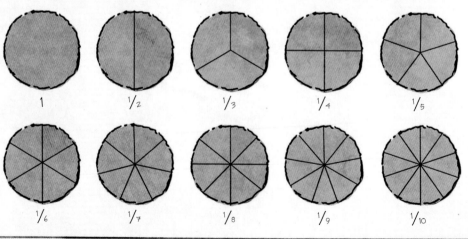

1   ¹⁄₂   ¹⁄₃   ¹⁄₄   ¹⁄₅

¹⁄₆   ¹⁄₇   ¹⁄₈   ¹⁄₉   ¹⁄₁₀

Parts of a group

Fractions can describe parts of a whole (as with the swamp grass pie below), but we can also use them to describe parts of a group. The mammoth has made a batch of four tasty swamp grass muffins. Three out of the four have no topping, while one has strawberry frosting. So we say that three-quarters (³/₄) of the batch are plain and one-quarter (¹/₄) have frosting.

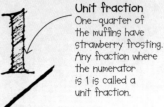

Unit fraction
One-quarter of the muffins have strawberry frosting. Any fraction where the numerator is 1 is called a unit fraction.

Three-quarters (³/₄) of the muffins have no topping

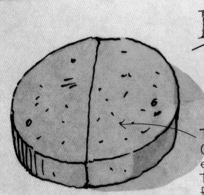
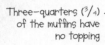

Two halves
Cutting the pie into 2 equal parts makes 2 halves. That's not enough slices for 8 hungry shrews.

Four quarters
Next, the shrew cuts the pie into 4 equal slices, or quarters—still not enough pieces to go around.

Eight eighths
Finally, the pie is divided into 8 equal parts, or eighths—an equal slice for each salivating shrew!

Numerator
The top number in a fraction is called the numerator. It tells you how many equal parts of the whole you have.

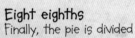

Denominator
This is the number below the dividing line. The denominator tells you how many equal parts the whole is divided into.

Types of fractions

Fractions where the number of parts is less than a whole are called proper fractions. Any fraction where the numerator is less than the denominator (see page 45) is a proper fraction. But sometimes we might want to use fractions to describe amounts that add up to more than one whole. We can write amounts like this either as improper fractions or as mixed numbers.

Pie party

The mammoth baker is serving up swamp grass pie to a party of young mammoths. Each gets half a pie. To describe the amount of pie there is in total, we can use a whole number alongside a proper fraction. This is known as a mixed number. Or we can use an improper fraction, where the numerator is larger than the denominator.

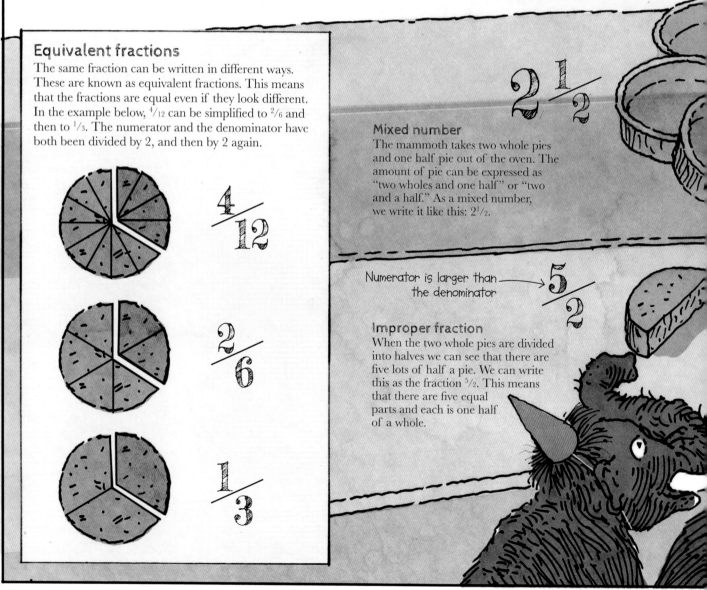

Equivalent fractions

The same fraction can be written in different ways. These are known as equivalent fractions. This means that the fractions are equal even if they look different. In the example below, $4/12$ can be simplified to $2/6$ and then to $1/3$. The numerator and the denominator have both been divided by 2, and then by 2 again.

$$\frac{4}{12}$$

$$\frac{2}{6}$$

$$\frac{1}{3}$$

Mixed number

The mammoth takes two whole pies and one half pie out of the oven. The amount of pie can be expressed as "two wholes and one half" or "two and a half." As a mixed number, we write it like this: $2^{1}/_{2}$.

$$2\frac{1}{2}$$

Numerator is larger than the denominator $\longrightarrow \frac{5}{2}$

Improper fraction

When the two whole pies are divided into halves we can see that there are five lots of half a pie. We can write this as the fraction $5/2$. This means that there are five equal parts and each is one half of a whole.

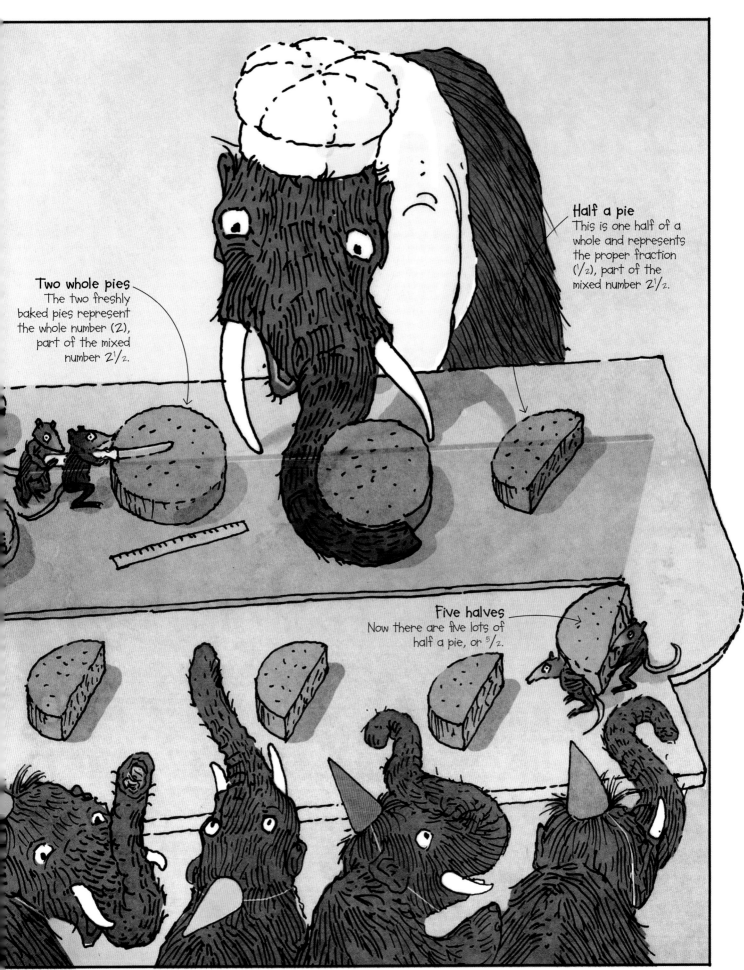

Two whole pies
The two freshly baked pies represent the whole number (2), part of the mixed number 2½.

Half a pie
This is one half of a whole and represents the proper fraction (½), part of the mixed number 2½.

Five halves
Now there are five lots of half a pie, or ⁵/₂.

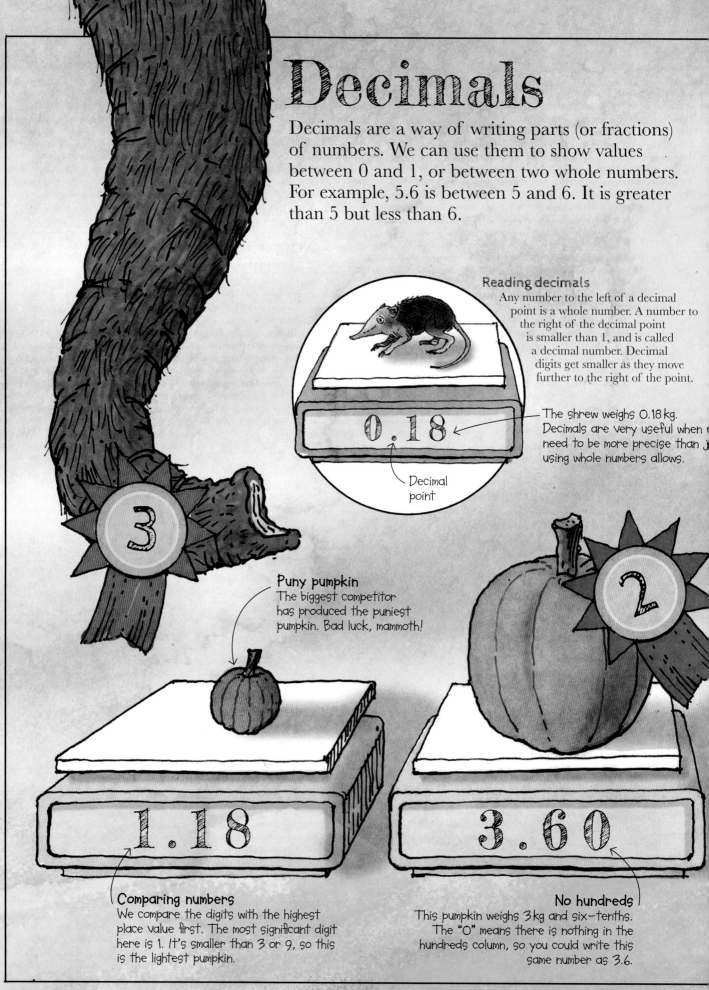

Decimals

Decimals are a way of writing parts (or fractions) of numbers. We can use them to show values between 0 and 1, or between two whole numbers. For example, 5.6 is between 5 and 6. It is greater than 5 but less than 6.

Reading decimals

Any number to the left of a decimal point is a whole number. A number to the right of the decimal point is smaller than 1, and is called a decimal number. Decimal digits get smaller as they move further to the right of the point.

The shrew weighs 0.18 kg. Decimals are very useful when need to be more precise than j using whole numbers allows.

0.18

Decimal point

Puny pumpkin

The biggest competitor has produced the puniest pumpkin. Bad luck, mammoth!

1.18

3.60

Comparing numbers

We compare the digits with the highest place value first. The most significant digit here is 1. It's smaller than 3 or 9, so this is the lightest pumpkin.

No hundreds

This pumpkin weighs 3 kg and six-tenths. The "0" means there is nothing in the hundreds column, so you could write this same number as 3.6.

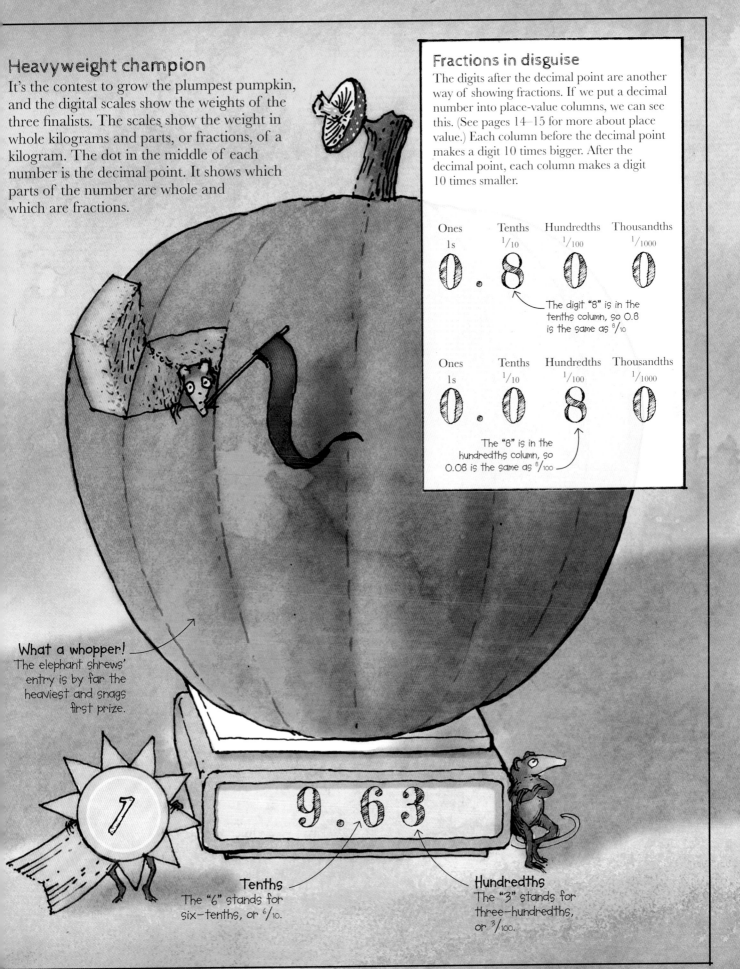

Heavyweight champion

It's the contest to grow the plumpest pumpkin, and the digital scales show the weights of the three finalists. The scales show the weight in whole kilograms and parts, or fractions, of a kilogram. The dot in the middle of each number is the decimal point. It shows which parts of the number are whole and which are fractions.

Fractions in disguise

The digits after the decimal point are another way of showing fractions. If we put a decimal number into place-value columns, we can see this. (See pages 14–15 for more about place value.) Each column before the decimal point makes a digit 10 times bigger. After the decimal point, each column makes a digit 10 times smaller.

Ones 1s	Tenths $1/10$	Hundredths $1/100$	Thousandths $1/1000$
0.	8	0	0

The digit "8" is in the tenths column, so 0.8 is the same as $^6/_{10}$

Ones 1s	Tenths $1/10$	Hundredths $1/100$	Thousandths $1/1000$
0.	0	8	0

The "8" is in the hundredths column, so 0.08 is the same as $^8/_{100}$

What a whopper!
The elephant shrews' entry is by far the heaviest and snags first prize.

9.63

Tenths
The "6" stands for six-tenths, or $^6/_{10}$.

Hundredths
The "3" stands for three-hundredths, or $^3/_{100}$.

Percentages

Percent means "per one-hundred," and that's exactly what a percentage is—a way of representing an amount as a number out of 100. Percentages are a really useful way of comparing different quantities. The symbol "%" is used to show a percentage.

Ready to launch

A crowd of elephant shrews has gathered to watch as one plucky mammoth boldly blasts off into space. There are 100 shrew spectators, which makes it easy to see how percentages work. But we can use percentages to compare all sorts of quantities, such as the lengths of the rocket's three sections. We simply split the total length into 100 parts in order to compare proportions.

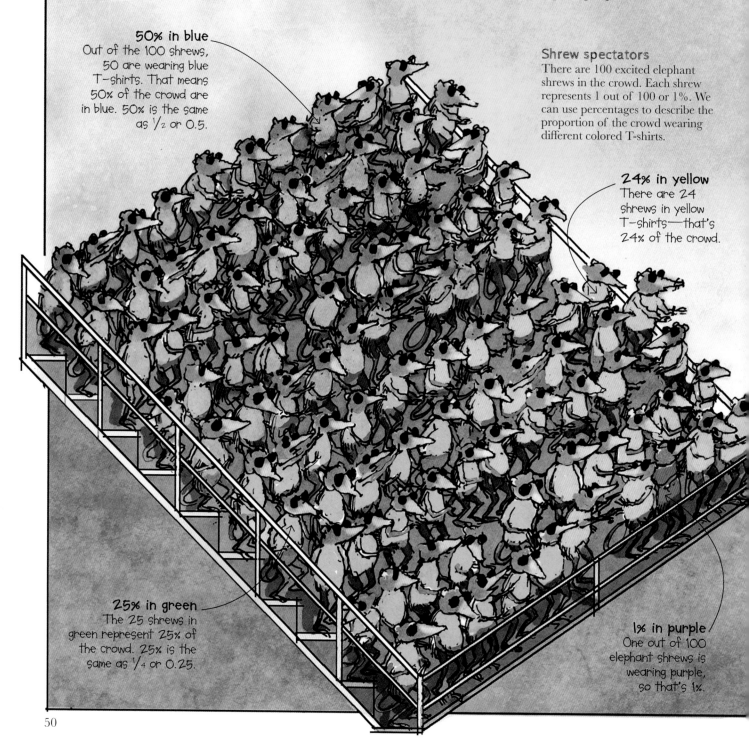

50% in blue
Out of the 100 shrews, 50 are wearing blue T-shirts. That means 50% of the crowd are in blue. 50% is the same as $\frac{1}{2}$ or 0.5.

Shrew spectators
There are 100 excited elephant shrews in the crowd. Each shrew represents 1 out of 100 or 1%. We can use percentages to describe the proportion of the crowd wearing different colored T-shirts.

24% in yellow
There are 24 shrews in yellow T-shirts—that's 24% of the crowd.

25% in green
The 25 shrews in green represent 25% of the crowd. 25% is the same as $\frac{1}{4}$ or 0.25.

1% in purple
One out of 100 elephant shrews is wearing purple, so that's 1%.

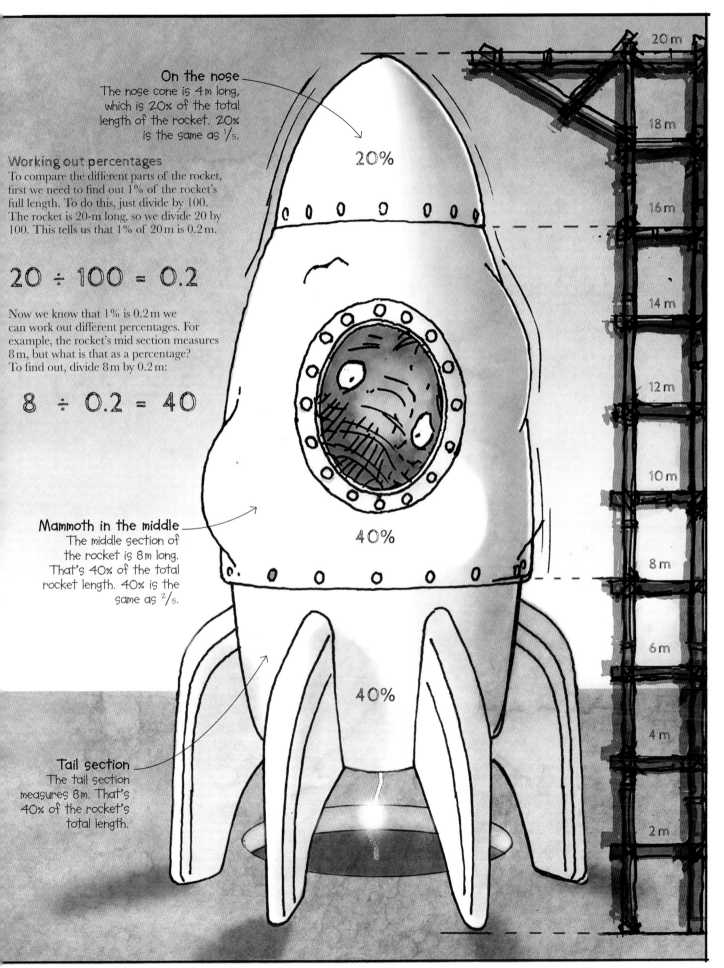

On the nose
The nose cone is 4 m long, which is 20% of the total length of the rocket. 20% is the same as $\frac{1}{5}$.

Working out percentages

To compare the different parts of the rocket, first we need to find out 1% of the rocket's full length. To do this, just divide by 100. The rocket is 20-m long, so we divide 20 by 100. This tells us that 1% of 20 m is 0.2 m.

$$20 \div 100 = 0.2$$

Now we know that 1% is 0.2 m we can work out different percentages. For example, the rocket's mid section measures 8 m, but what is that as a percentage? To find out, divide 8 m by 0.2 m:

$$8 \div 0.2 = 40$$

20%

40%

40%

Mammoth in the middle
The middle section of the rocket is 8 m long. That's 40% of the total rocket length. 40% is the same as $\frac{2}{5}$.

Tail section
The tail section measures 8 m. That's 40% of the rocket's total length.

20 m

18 m

16 m

14 m

12 m

10 m

8 m

6 m

4 m

2 m

Ratio

When you want to compare two numbers or quantities, ratio is the perfect math tool for the job. It's a way of showing how much bigger or smaller one amount is than the other. For example, when mixing colors like these fashion-conscious mammoths, you might want to describe how much of one ingredient there should be compared to another.

1 to 1
First, the shrews mix one pot of blue and one pot of red dye. The ratio of blue to red is 1 to 1. We write a ratio as two numbers separated by a colon (two dots), like this—1:1.

1 to 2
Now the shrew has added another pot of red, so the ratio of blue to red is 1 to 2, or 1:2.

1 to 3
After adding a final pot of red, the shrews have found the perfect purple. The ratio of blue to red is 1 to 3, or 1:3.

Mixing it up
The shrews are mixing blue and red dye in a bucket until they find their ideal purple. By adding more red pots until they get the color they want, they are also changing the ratio of blue dye to red.

The right ratio
Everybody wants to be seen in this season's on-trend shade, "gorgeous grape." First, the elephant shrews mix up the right amounts of blue and red dye to make the perfect shade of purple. To fill the mammoths' pool they will need a lot more dye, but they must keep the same ratio or they'll end up with the wrong shade of purple for the pool party.

Purple pool party
The mammoths and shrews take a dip in the purple pool then parade their new dye job.

Making more
To fill the pool, it takes 10 pots of blue dye and 30 pots of red. That's a ratio of 10:30. If we simplify the ratio by dividing each number by 10, we see that 10:30 is the same as 1:3. For every one pot of blue dye, three pots of red have been added.

Pretty in purple
Purple is the mammoths' favorite color. They like it more than blue or red.

10 pots of blue
More pots of dye are used to fill the pool than the bucket, but the ratio of blue to red is the same.

1:3

Proportion
Proportion is comparing an amount to the whole amount that it is part of. It describes how much of the whole is taken up by a particular bit. For example, to fill the pool the shrews used 10 pots of blue dye and 30 pots of red, making a total of 40. So 10 out of 40 pots were blue. We write this as the fraction $^{10}/_{40}$, then simplify it to say that $^{1}/_{4}$ of the dye in the pool is blue. Can you work out what proportion was red?

$^{1}/_{4}$ of the dye was blue

You can find the solution on page 160.

Scaling down

When you take a photograph, the image is a scaled-down version of the real thing. It is smaller, but in the same proportions. Say this mammoth is 300 cm high and its snapshot image fits into a screen measuring 12 cm. 300 divided by 12 equals 25, which gives a scale factor of 25. On the screen, every part of the image has been scaled down to $\frac{1}{25}$ (or one-twenty-fifth) of the mammoth's actual size.

Scaling

Making something smaller or larger while keeping all of its parts in proportion with each other is called scaling. This means that all parts are enlarged or reduced by the same amount. To enlarge something to scale, you multiply its measurements, such as length and width. To reduce something to scale, you divide the measurements.

Scaling up
The height of the statue is four times higher than the sitting shrew.

Scale factor
The number that an object has been multiplied or divided by is known as the scale factor. To find the scale factor, the heights of the shrew and the statue are measured. The statue is four times larger than the shrew, so the scale factor is 4.

Statue subject
The elephant shrew has to sit very still while posing for the statue!

4

3

2

1

Scaled-up statue

The mammoth is sculpting a statue of an elephant shrew that is much bigger than the shrew itself. Sitting down on the plinth, the shrew measures 10 in (25 cm) high. The mammoth is making a statue that is 40 in (100 cm) high, so every part of the shrew statue will be four times larger than real life.

Measuring up
All parts of the real shrew must be multiplied by 4 to keep the statue in proportion.

Puzzling patterns and super sequences

Sequences

Patterns crop up everywhere in math—often even the most random-seeming groups of shapes or numbers are linked. When we put numbers or shapes in a certain order, they make a sequence. Each number or shape in the sequence is called a term and the set pattern that they follow is called a rule.

Laundry lines

The mammoth makes boring chores more fun by hanging laundry in different sequences, each following a different rule to get from term to term. A sequence can be based on addition, subtraction, multiplication, or division, or a mix of all four of these.

Shape sequence

The woolens make a sequence of shapes, which goes like this: sock, hat, sock, mittens. The sequence then repeats itself, starting again with a sock.

Stick to the rule
Each shirt number is two more than the previous number.

+2

Number sequence

The number on each shirt is two more than the one before. So the sequence rule is "add two to each term to get the next term." We write the sequence like this: 2, 4, 6, 8 .... Each term is separated by a comma. The dots at the end show that the sequence can carry on.

What's the next shirt in this subtraction sequence? See page 160 for the solution.

2

4

14   11   8   5

Adding to a sequence

With sequences, once you've worked out the rule, you can use it to find the next term in your sequence, and then the one after that, and so on. The first number in a sequence is called the first term. Any term that you don't yet know is called the nth term—"n" stands for the value you haven't worked out. In this shape sequence, the rule is "add a side to a shape to get the next shape." Can you use the rule to draw the shape that will be the nth term?

First shape has 3 sides

1st term   2nd term   3rd term   4th term

7th shape has 9 sides

5th term   6th term   7th term   nth term

What's next?
Using the rule, we can work out that the term after 8 will be 10. Can you work out the next 5 terms after 10?

+2

6

8

Prime numbers

A prime is a whole number bigger than 1 that can't be divided by any other whole number except for itself and 1. These special numbers are sometimes called the building blocks of all other numbers. But how do you know if a number is a prime? The mammoths have built a machine for this very purpose.

PRIME NUMBERS

1	2	3	4	5	6	7	8	9	10
11	12	13	14	15	16	17	18	19	20
21	22	23	24	25	26	27	28	29	30
31	32	33	34	35	36	37	38	39	40
41	42	43	44	45	46	47	48	49	50
51	52	53	54	55	56	57	58	59	60
61	62	63	64	65	66	67	68	69	70
71	72	73	74	75	76	77	78	79	80
81	82	83	84	85	86	87	88	89	90
91	92	93	94	95	96	97	98	99	100

No pattern
This table shows all the primes to 100 shaded in pink. There is no pattern to them—they seem to occur at random.

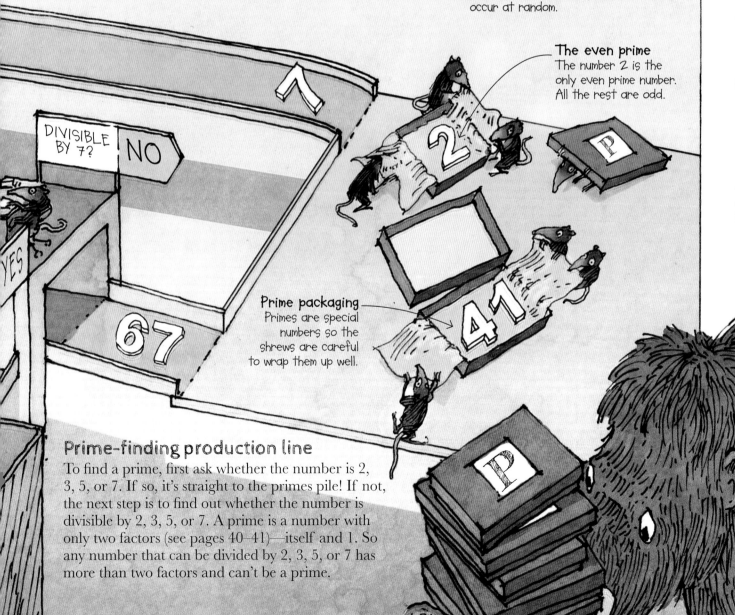

The even prime
The number 2 is the only even prime number. All the rest are odd.

Prime packaging
Primes are special numbers so the shrews are careful to wrap them up well.

DIVISIBLE BY 7? NO

YES

Prime-finding production line
To find a prime, first ask whether the number is 2, 3, 5, or 7. If so, it's straight to the primes pile! If not, the next step is to find out whether the number is divisible by 2, 3, 5, or 7. A prime is a number with only two factors (see pages 40–41)—itself and 1. So any number that can be divided by 2, 3, 5, or 7 has more than two factors and can't be a prime.

Square numbers

When you multiply a whole number by itself, the result is called a square number. For example, 3 multiplied by 3 is 9, so we say that 9 is the square of 3. Square numbers are so-called because you can show each number as an actual square. We write square numbers using a small 2, like this: 3^2.

Potato prints

The elephant shrews have been busy chopping potatoes into rectangular pieces with square faces at each end. The mammoths are using these to print a sequence of larger and larger square numbers. You can find the value of each of these square numbers by counting the stamps in each square.

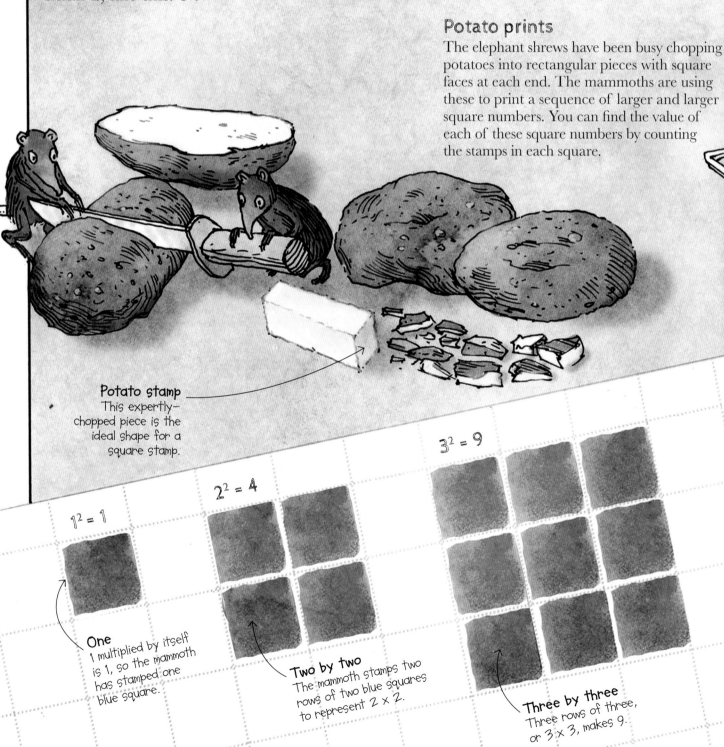

Potato stamp
This expertly–chopped piece is the ideal shape for a square stamp.

$1^2 = 1$

One
1 multiplied by itself is 1, so the mammoth has stamped one blue square.

$2^2 = 4$

Two by two
The mammoth stamps two rows of two blue squares to represent 2 x 2.

$3^2 = 9$

Three by three
Three rows of three, or 3 x 3, makes 9.

Square roots

The number that you multiply by itself to find a square number is known as that square number's root, or its square root. All square numbers have square roots. Square numbers and square roots are opposites of each other. For example, 16 is the square of 4, so 4 is the square root of 16. The symbol for a square root is √.

Square

5 is the square root of 25

5

25 is the square of 5

25

Square root

Ink pad
The mammoth dips the potatoes in the ink before using them to stamp the grid.

$5^2 = ?$

$4^2 = 16$

Five squared?
The mammoth is still stamping out 5^2. How many blue squares will there be once the mammoth has finished? (See page 160 for the answer.)

Four squared
The fourth square number has four stamps in four rows, for a total of 16 stamps.

Cube numbers

A cube number is a whole number that is multiplied by itself, then by itself again. It gets its name because a cube number can be shown as a cube shape. The first cube number (1 x 1 x 1) is one cube long, one cube high, and one cube deep. The next cube number (2 x 2 x 2) is two cubes long, two cubes high, and two cubes deep.

Making cubes

While the mammoth enjoys a relaxing break, the elephant shrews are busy making sugar cubes. They sculpt each sugar lump into a small cube (a 3D shape with square faces) and then stack them up so that they make ever-larger cube structures.

Cubes in a sequence

The shrews have arranged these sugar cubes to show the sequence of cube numbers. Multiplying the number of sugar cubes in each stack's height, width, and length gives each cube number in the sequence. Cube numbers are shown with a small 3 beside the number, like this: 1^3.

Unit
Each sugar cube stands for one unit.

1^3
This sugar cube is one unit long, one unit high, and one unit wide:
$1 \times 1 \times 1 = 1$.

2^3
This cube is two units long, two units high, and two units wide:
$2 \times 2 \times 2 = 8$.

3^3
This cube is three units long, three units high, and three units wide:
$3 \times 3 \times 3 = 27$.

4^3

When completed, this cube will be four units long, four units high, and four units wide:
$4 \times 4 \times 4 = 64$.

Get the power

The small 3 that indicates a cube number is called an index (or indices if there are more than one), or power. A power is a quick way of showing how many times a number has been multiplied by itself. For example, a number multiplied by itself twice, known as a square number, has been multiplied to the power of 2: $2 \times 2 = 2^2$.

A number multiplied by itself three times, known as a cube number, has been multiplied to the power of 3: $2 \times 2 \times 2 = 2^3$.

$$5^3 = 5 \times 5 \times 5$$

$$= 125$$

The number 5 has been multiplied by itself three times, or to the power of 3

Here, the index number is 10. It has only increased by 7, but the product is now more than 9 million!

$$5^{10} = 5 \times 5 \times 5 \times 5 \times 5 \times 5 \times 5 \times 5 \times 5 \times 5$$

$$= 9{,}765{,}625$$

Fibonacci sequence

There is a very interesting sequence in math, named after a 13th-century Italian mathematician—it is called the Fibonacci sequence. Each number in the sequence is found by adding the previous two together. This sequence of numbers can be used to draw a spiral, as the elephant shrews are finding out.

1 + 1   1 + 2   2 + 3   3 + 5   5 + 8   8 + 13   13 + 21

1   1   2   3   5   8   13   21   34...

Sequence starts at 1

A special spiral

Inspired by the curl of the mammoth's trunk, the elephant shrews are using the Fibonacci sequence to build a hair-raising spiral slide. To get the spiral shape, first they turn the sequence of numbers into squares. The length of each square's sides represents the terms in the sequence.

Step two

The second term in the sequence is 1, so the shrews put another square down alongside the first. The third term is 2, so the shrews then lay down a box whose sides are 2 squares long.

Another square
The second term is 1, so another single square is added.

Step one

The first term in the sequence is 1, so the shrew lays out one square on the ground. The shrew draws a quarter circle connecting the square's opposite corners.

Starting to spiral
Each time the shrews make a square, they draw a quarter circle to connect the corners.

Step three
The grid is beginning to grow. The next term is 3, so the shrews need to add a box with sides 3 squares long.

Each new square's sides are the length of the previous two put together

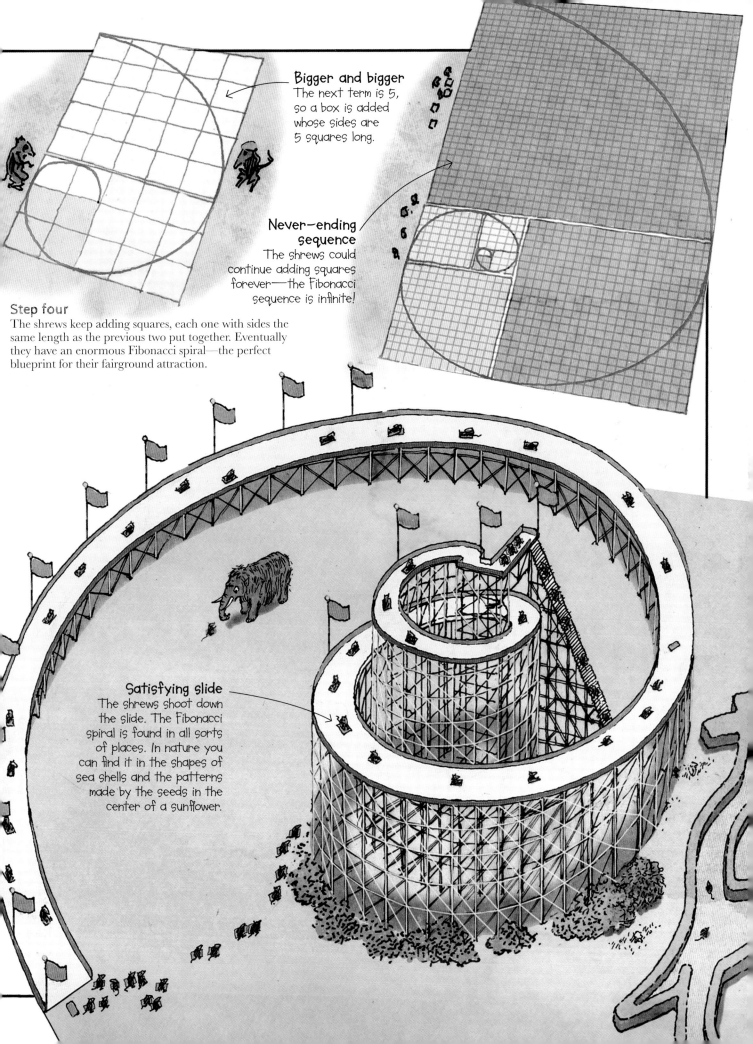

Bigger and bigger
The next term is 5, so a box is added whose sides are 5 squares long.

Never-ending sequence
The shrews could continue adding squares forever—the Fibonacci sequence is infinite!

Step four
The shrews keep adding squares, each one with sides the same length as the previous two put together. Eventually they have an enormous Fibonacci spiral—the perfect blueprint for their fairground attraction.

Satisfying slide
The shrews shoot down the slide. The Fibonacci spiral is found in all sorts of places. In nature you can find it in the shapes of sea shells and the patterns made by the seeds in the center of a sunflower.

Magic shapes

When you put shapes and numbers together you can make some tricky challenges. One of these is the magic triangle. To solve this three-sided riddle, the numbers along each side of the triangle must add up to the magic number that sits in the center.

Pool, interrupted

The mammoths are enjoying a game of pool on the lawn when the elephant shrews decide to borrow their balls to construct a magic triangle. Still, at least there's a new game to play as the woolly ones puzzle out which numbered ball should go in which hole.

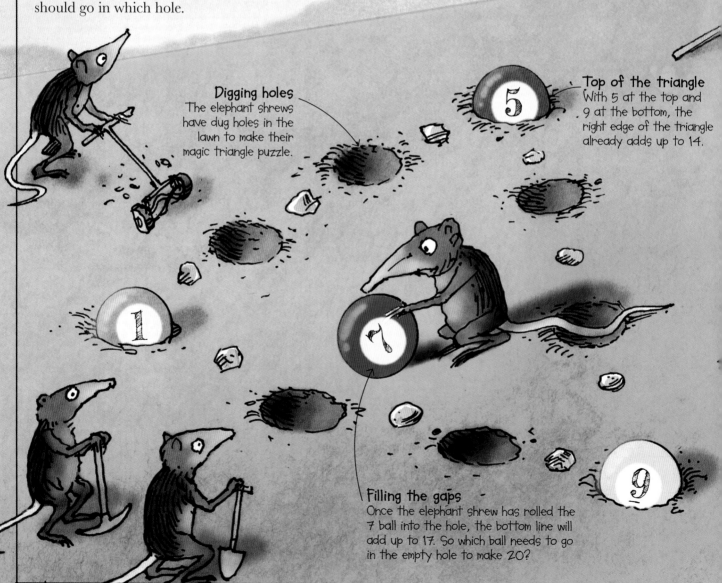

Digging holes
The elephant shrews have dug holes in the lawn to make their magic triangle puzzle.

Top of the triangle
With 5 at the top and 9 at the bottom, the right edge of the triangle already adds up to 14.

Filling the gaps
Once the elephant shrew has rolled the 7 ball into the hole, the bottom line will add up to 17. So which ball needs to go in the empty hole to make 20?

Magic squares

Triangles aren't the only shapes to contain perplexing patterns. In a magic square, every column, row, and diagonal line adds up to the same number. In fact, you can also get this number, called the magic sum, if you add all four numbers in the corners, or the four in the center. According to legend, the first magic square was discovered more than 4,000 years ago by a Chinese emperor.

Finding the magic sum

In the magic square below, the magic sum is 34. It uses each number between 1 and 16 only once and every vertical, horizontal, and diagonal line adds up to 34.

16	3	2	13
5	10	11	8
9	6	7	12
4	15	14	1

The four numbers in the corners also add up to 34.

Solve the square

Can you solve this magic square by filling in the missing numbers? The magic sum is 111 and each number between 1 and 36 must be used only once. Start by looking for lines with only one missing number.

	18				23
	25		27	22	31
34	9	1	10		21
6		30	28		16
	14	29	8	20	
	15	35	17	13	

You can find the solution on page 160.

Order of four

There are four spaces on each of this triangle's sides so it is called a four-order triangle.

Magic number: 20

20

Use the following numbers:
1, 2, 3, 4, 5, 6, 7, 8, 9

20 is plenty

The number in the center of this magic triangle is 20. Can you use the numbers on the balls to make the sides of the triangle add up to 20? You can only use each number once. To give you a start the shrews have already rolled three of the balls into place.

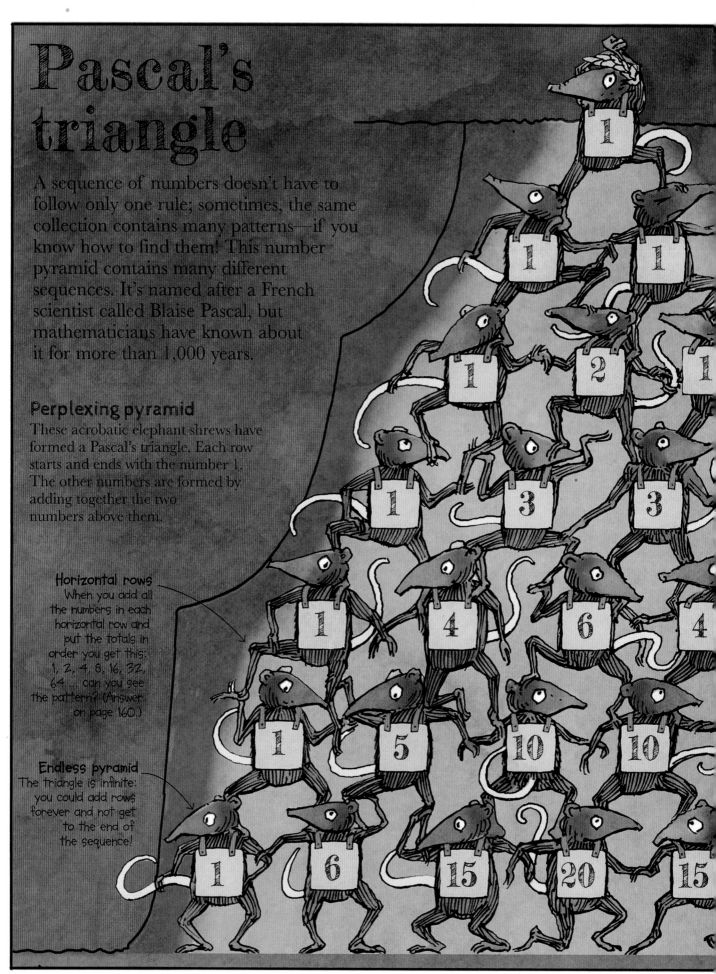

Pascal's triangle

A sequence of numbers doesn't have to follow only one rule; sometimes, the same collection contains many patterns—if you know how to find them! This number pyramid contains many different sequences. It's named after a French scientist called Blaise Pascal, but mathematicians have known about it for more than 1,000 years.

Perplexing pyramid

These acrobatic elephant shrews have formed a Pascal's triangle. Each row starts and ends with the number 1. The other numbers are formed by adding together the two numbers above them.

Horizontal rows
When you add all the numbers in each horizontal row and put the totals in order you get this: 1, 2, 4, 8, 16, 32, 64 ... can you see the pattern? (Answer on page 160.)

Endless pyramid
The triangle is infinite: you could add rows forever and not get to the end of the sequence!

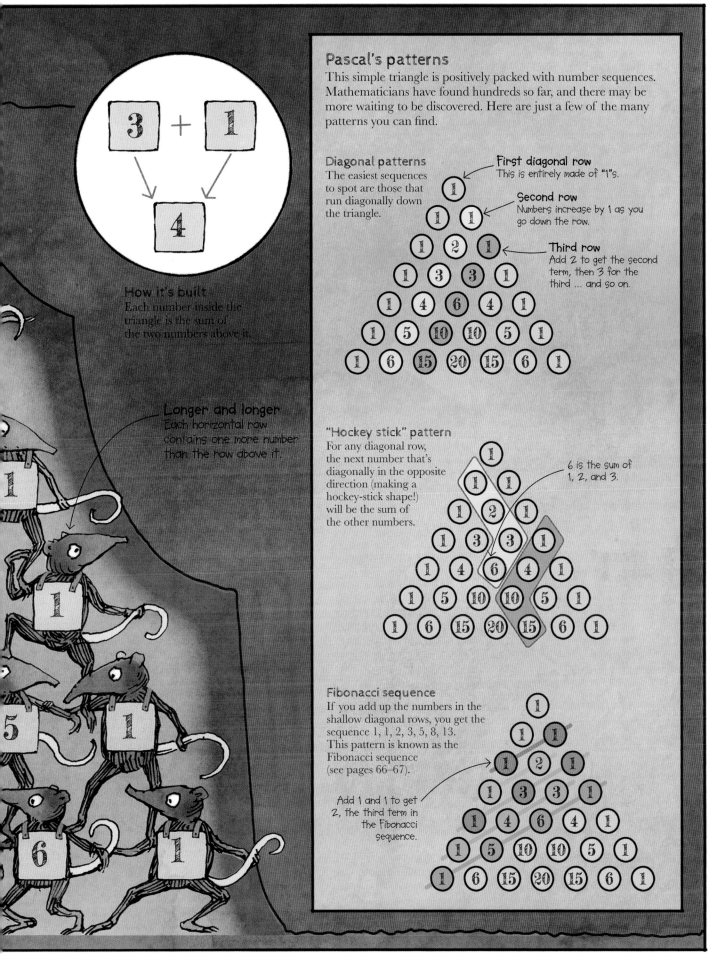

How it's built
Each number inside the triangle is the sum of the two numbers above it.

Longer and longer
Each horizontal row contains one more number than the row above it.

Pascal's patterns

This simple triangle is positively packed with number sequences. Mathematicians have found hundreds so far, and there may be more waiting to be discovered. Here are just a few of the many patterns you can find.

Diagonal patterns
The easiest sequences to spot are those that run diagonally down the triangle.

First diagonal row
This is entirely made of "1"s.

Second row
Numbers increase by 1 as you go down the row.

Third row
Add 2 to get the second term, then 3 for the third ... and so on.

"Hockey stick" pattern
For any diagonal row, the next number that's diagonally in the opposite direction (making a hockey-stick shape!) will be the sum of the other numbers.

6 is the sum of 1, 2, and 3.

Fibonacci sequence
If you add up the numbers in the shallow diagonal rows, you get the sequence 1, 1, 2, 3, 5, 8, 13. This pattern is known as the Fibonacci sequence (see pages 66–67).

Add 1 and 1 to get 2, the third term in the Fibonacci sequence.

Coded invite

The shrouded shrew sets the cipher wheel so that A on the inner ring aligns with E on the outer ring. Each letter of the shrew's message is substituted with the letter 4 places ahead of it in the alphabet. The coded message is then dispatched into the night.

Coded message

If you know the rule, you can decode the message, but to the uninitiated this message looks like gobbledygook.

Pigeon mail

The coded invites are sent out while the mammoth is fast asleep.

TEVXC JSV
QEQQSXL
EX RSSR

Key

To decode the message, the reader must line up the two alphabets in the same way the first shrew did.

A=E

Wheely useful

The shrew could encode the message just using the rule "use the letter 4 places ahead," but the cipher wheel makes it much quicker.

Codes

A code is a system of letters, numbers, or words that are used to represent other letters, numbers, and words. Once a message has been encoded, it looks like a meaningless jumble. Only those in the know will be able to crack the code.

Caesar cipher

Top secret plans are afoot. To keep their communications classified, the elephant shrews are using a code called a Caesar cipher, or Caesar shift, where each letter is replaced with another. The simple trick is to shift the alphabet one or more places. For example, replace each letter with the one that comes after it in the alphabet, so that "a" becomes "b" and so on. The shrews are using a cipher wheel to help with their secret scheme.

Binary code

Numbers can also be used to make codes. Binary code is a code that uses only two digits: 0 and 1. Every letter, number, and symbol is represented as a series of 0s and 1s. For example, the letter A would be encoded as 01000001. When digital information is sent out from a computer, it is encoded as a stream of these binary 0s and 1s. The receiving computer translates the binary digits back into the letters and symbols that we recognize.

Spinning wheel
The outer ring moves around, so the shrews can reset the wheel—aligning the letters differently and creating a new cipher each time.

Ring the changes
The letters on the outer ring are the cipher. The ones on the inner ring are the "real" letters.

Cipher wheel
Using this tool makes it much easier to decode the message. All the shrews have to do is use the key to align the wheel correctly.

Party time!
The code is cracked and it's time to celebrate. Happy birthday, mammoth!

Decoding the message
The shrews set their device then get to work decoding. Each letter on the message is located on the outside circle of the device, then swapped for the matching letter on the inside.

PARTY FOR MAMMOTH AT NOON

Maps, maneuvers, and movements

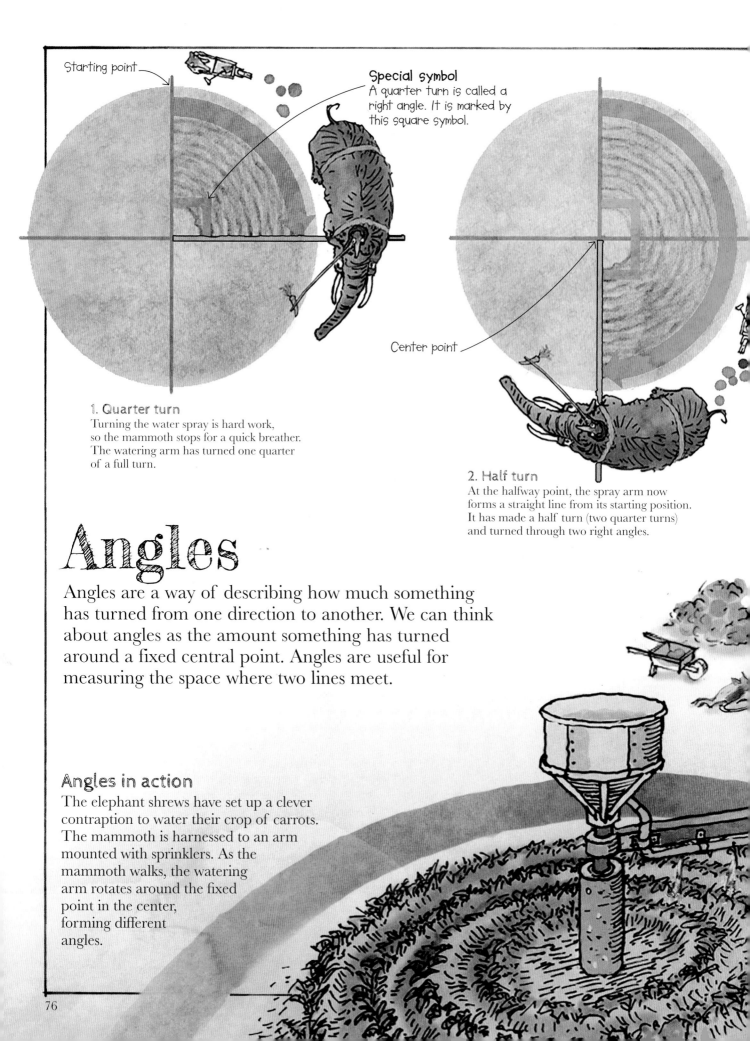

Starting point

Center point

1. Quarter turn
Turning the water spray is hard work, so the mammoth stops for a quick breather. The watering arm has turned one quarter of a full turn.

2. Half turn
At the halfway point, the spray arm now forms a straight line from its starting position. It has made a half turn (two quarter turns) and turned through two right angles.

Angles

Angles are a way of describing how much something has turned from one direction to another. We can think about angles as the amount something has turned around a fixed central point. Angles are useful for measuring the space where two lines meet.

Angles in action
The elephant shrews have set up a clever contraption to water their crop of carrots. The mammoth is harnessed to an arm mounted with sprinklers. As the mammoth walks, the watering arm rotates around the fixed point in the center, forming different angles.

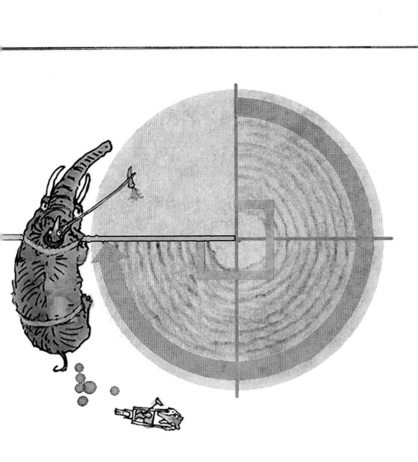

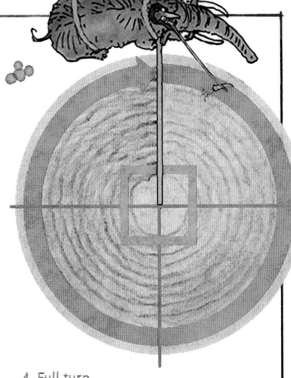

4. Full turn

Job done! The mammoth has now turned the arm all the way back around to the beginning. It has made four quarter turns—or one full turn.

3. Three-quarter turn

Almost there! The mammoth has made it through another quarter turn and stops again for a rest. The arm has made a three-quarter turn.

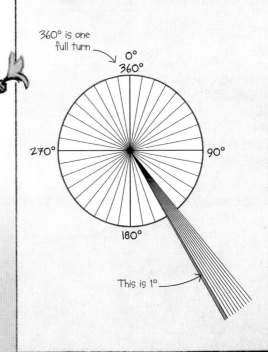

Measuring with degrees

Angles are measured using units called degrees. We use this circle symbol to show degrees: °. A full turn is divided up into 360 equal-size degrees. That means that 1 degree is equal to $1/360$ of a full turn. A quarter turn (right angle) is 90° and a half turn is 180°.

360° is one full turn

0°
360°

270°   90°

180°

This is 1°

Types of angle

We can measure an angle between any two lines that meet at a vertex (another word for a corner). The two lines that meet are called the angle's arms, and we mark the angle between them with a curved line called an arc. Some of the most important kinds of angles are named according to their size.

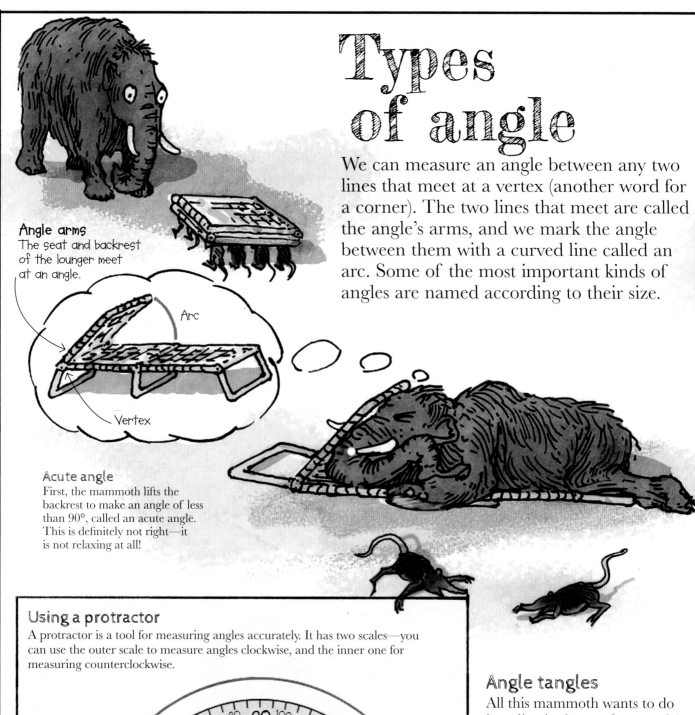

Angle arms
The seat and backrest of the lounger meet at an angle.

Arc

Vertex

Acute angle
First, the mammoth lifts the backrest to make an angle of less than 90°, called an acute angle. This is definitely not right—it is not relaxing at all!

Using a protractor
A protractor is a tool for measuring angles accurately. It has two scales—you can use the outer scale to measure angles clockwise, and the inner one for measuring counterclockwise.

150°

30°

0° on the protractor lines up with one arm of the angle you want to measure

Center of the protractor sits on the angle's vertex

Angle tangles
All this mammoth wants to do is recline in the sun for a restful snooze, but unfolding the lounger to the perfect angle is proving a struggle. The mammoth tussles with the lounger, lifting the backrest into different positions, and creates four different kinds of angles between the bed and the backrest. But which is the best angle for the job?

Right angle

The mammoth pulls the backrest up a bit further, but still can't get comfortable! The lounger has made an angle of 90°, called a right angle.

Right angle

Angle greater than 90°

Obtuse angle

This is much better. The backrest is now at an angle that is greater than 90° but less than 180°. This is called an obtuse angle.

Angle greater than 180°

Reflex angle

Now it has gone too far! The mammoth has pushed the backrest right down to make an angle greater than 180°, called a reflex angle.

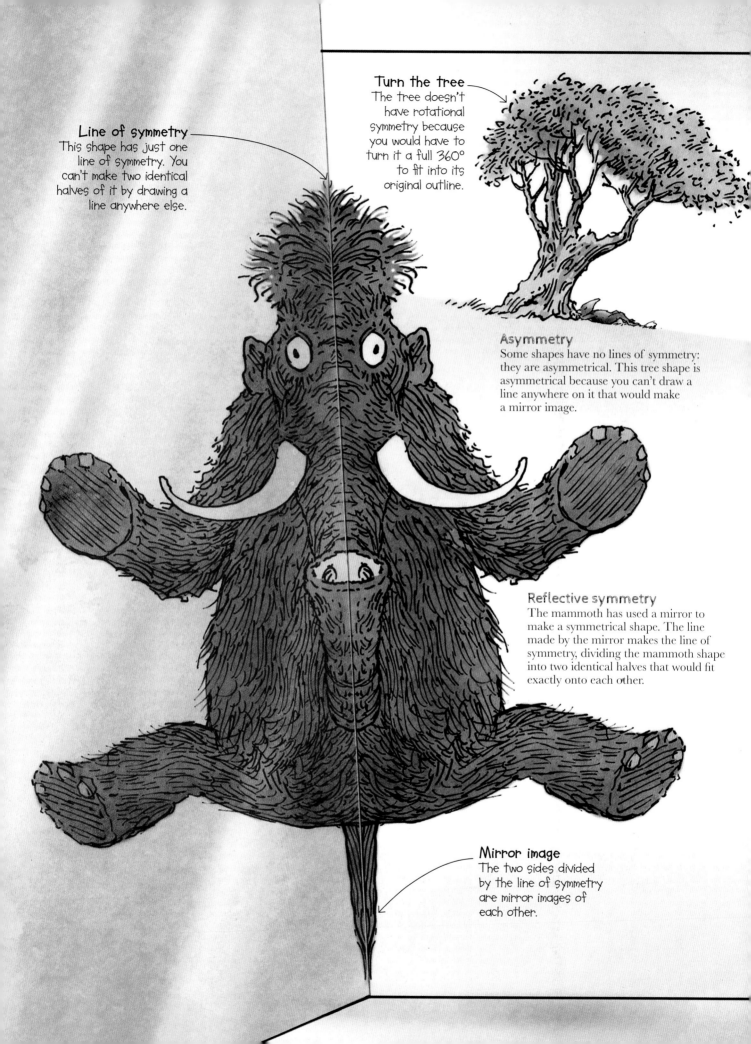

Line of symmetry
This shape has just one line of symmetry. You can't make two identical halves of it by drawing a line anywhere else.

Turn the tree
The tree doesn't have rotational symmetry because you would have to turn it a full 360° to fit into its original outline.

Asymmetry
Some shapes have no lines of symmetry: they are asymmetrical. This tree shape is asymmetrical because you can't draw a line anywhere on it that would make a mirror image.

Reflective symmetry
The mammoth has used a mirror to make a symmetrical shape. The line made by the mirror makes the line of symmetry, dividing the mammoth shape into two identical halves that would fit exactly onto each other.

Mirror image
The two sides divided by the line of symmetry are mirror images of each other.

Symmetry

A shape or an object has symmetry if you can draw a line through it to make two identical halves, just like mirror images of each other. This is called reflective symmetry. Shapes can have another type of symmetry, too. If you can rotate a shape around a center point so that it fits into its original outline, then it has rotational symmetry.

Nature's symmetry
A butterfly's wings are mirror images of each other, so it has one line of symmetry.

Finding symmetry

To find out whether a shape has reflective symmetry, imagine folding it in half. If the shape is symmetrical, the two halves will be a perfect match. To see whether a shape has rotational symmetry, imagine turning it around a central point or axis. The number of times the shape fits perfectly into its original outline in one full turn is called its order of rotational symmetry.

Quarter turns
Each time the shape makes a quarter turn, it fits perfectly into its original outline.

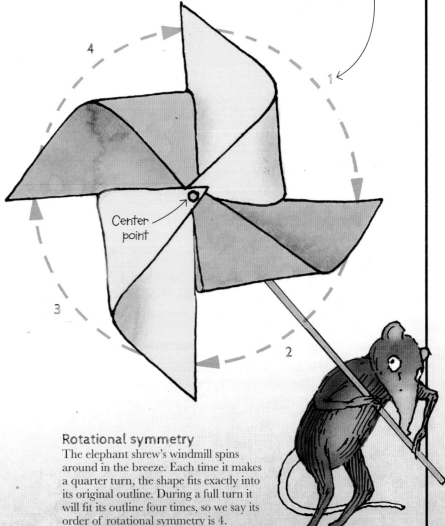

Center point

Lines of symmetry

Here are the lines of symmetry for some 2D shapes. Shapes can have one, two, or many lines of symmetry. A circle is unique, because any line that divides it though its center is a line of symmetry—so it has an infinite number.

Isosceles triangle
One line of symmetry

Rectangle
Two lines of symmetry

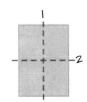

Equilateral triangle
Three lines of symmetry

Regular pentagon
Five lines of symmetry

Regular hexagon
Six lines of symmetry

Circle
Unlimited lines of symmetry

Rotational symmetry

The elephant shrew's windmill spins around in the breeze. Each time it makes a quarter turn, the shape fits exactly into its original outline. During a full turn it will fit its outline four times, so we say its order of rotational symmetry is 4.

Movement →
Translated shapes can go up, down, left, or right.

1. Translation
If an object is moved to a new position without changing its shape or size, this is called translation. The mammoth has leapt into the air and has kept the same shape, showing the translation of a shape.

2. Reflection
If an object is moved so that it makes a new, mirror image of the original object, this transformation is called reflection. Here, the mammoth and its shape in the mirror are on opposite sides of a straight line of reflection.

Transformations

In math, a change to the size or position of a shape is called a transformation. Shapes can be moved in many ways, but the three most common transformations are translation, reflection, and rotation. This dancing mammoth demonstrates all three while practicing perfect pirouettes.

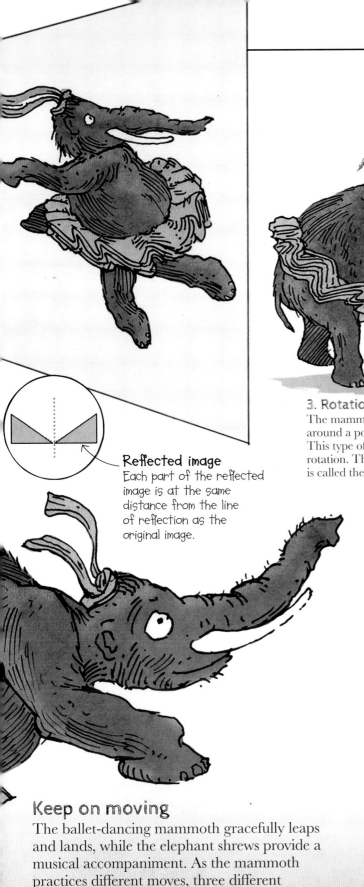

Center of rotation
This is the point around which the mammoth has turned.

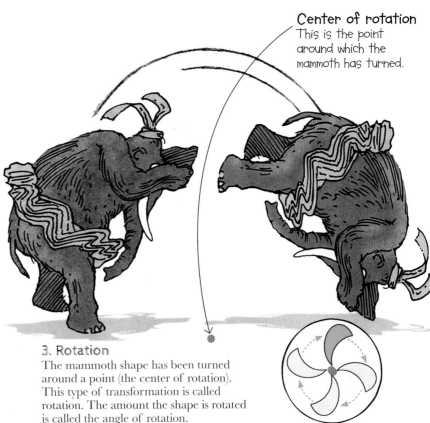

3. Rotation
The mammoth shape has been turned around a point (the center of rotation). This type of transformation is called rotation. The amount the shape is rotated is called the angle of rotation.

Reflected image
Each part of the reflected image is at the same distance from the line of reflection as the original image.

Tessellations
Translation can be used to make patterns called tessellations. These use identical shapes that fit together with no gaps between them and no overlapping. Identical quadrilaterals, triangles, and hexagons can always tessellate. Tessellated shapes can also be called tiles, and the arranging of shapes is known as tiling. In the picture below, the red and white mammoths have been translated diagonally so that they tessellate.

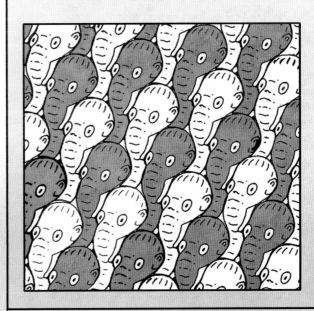

Keep on moving
The ballet-dancing mammoth gracefully leaps and lands, while the elephant shrews provide a musical accompaniment. As the mammoth practices different moves, three different transformations of shape take place.

Maps

The mammoths and elephant shrews are on an expedition to find a famous field where the plumpest pumpkins grow. They need to avoid hazards along the way, such as swamps, quarries, and murky lakes. What they need is a map—and the know-how to read it, of course.

How do maps work?

A grid divides the map into equal-size squares. The squares are labeled horizontally and vertically so that each has its own unique combination of letters and numbers. These are the square's coordinates.

Vertical axis
The squares down the sides are marked with numbers.

TUSK RIVER

PUMPKIN LANE

LAKE PLEISTOCENE

Pumpkin patch
Did you get it right? The parachuting shrew is aiming for square E10.

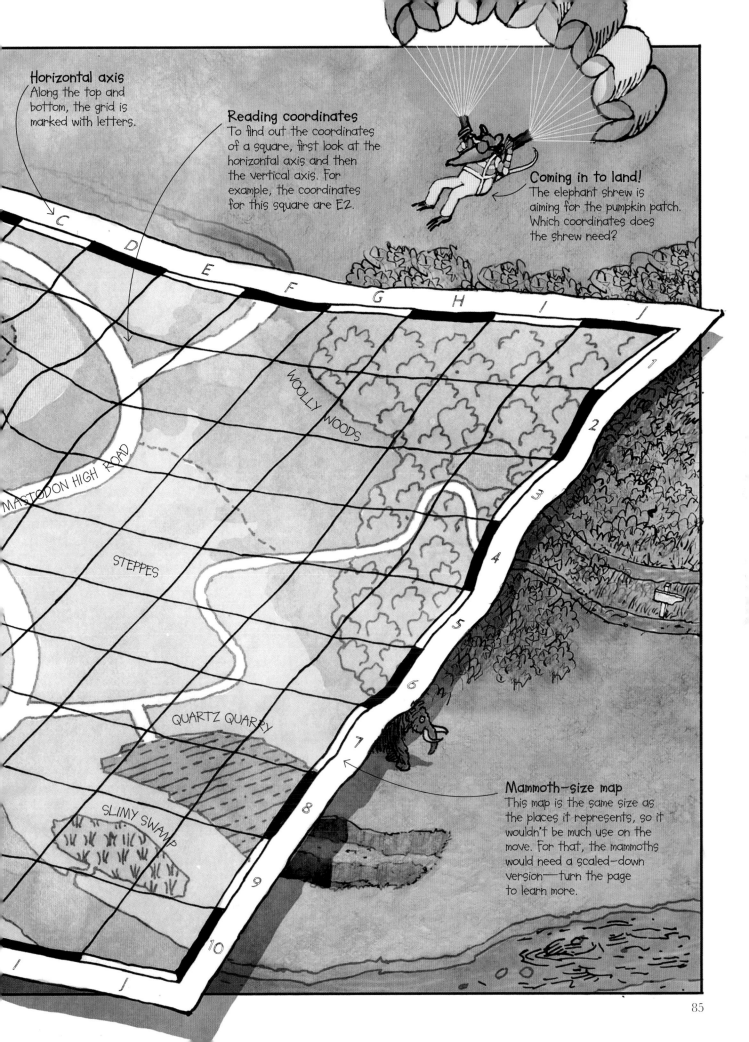

Horizontal axis
Along the top and bottom, the grid is marked with letters.

Reading coordinates
To find out the coordinates of a square, first look at the horizontal axis and then the vertical axis. For example, the coordinates for this square are E2.

Coming in to land!
The elephant shrew is aiming for the pumpkin patch. Which coordinates does the shrew need?

MASTODON HIGH ROAD

WOOLLY WOODS

STEPPES

QUARTZ QUARRY

SLIMY SWAMP

Mammoth-size map
This map is the same size as the places it represents, so it wouldn't be much use on the move. For that, the mammoths would need a scaled-down version—turn the page to learn more.

Map scales

A life-size map is not much use—it would be too big to carry around and use easily! Maps are scaled-down versions of real places. This means that places and the distances between them have all been reduced by the same amount. A map has exactly the same proportions as the real location it represents, it's just smaller.

Pinpointing the pumpkins

The elephant shrews have come to meet their parachuting friend at the pumpkin patch. Their map shows the same location as the one on pages 84–85, but it has been scaled down (see pages 54–55). The pumpkin patch, which takes up one whole grid square, measures 10 m across. On the shrews' map, this is drawn as 1 cm.

Scaling down
The proportions of the map are exactly the same as the life-size version. Everything has gotten smaller by the same amount.

Measuring up
The shrews measure a grid square and find it is 1 cm wide.

Scale bar
This shows that 1 cm on the map represents 10 m (1,000 cm) on the ground. So the scale is 1 cm:10 m or 1:1,000.

Choosing a scale

A map's scale is written as a ratio, which tells you how many units of a distance in real life are equal to one unit on the map. Different maps use different scales, depending on what they need to show. Maps with a large scale, such as the shrews' 1 cm:10 m map, can show more detail but won't cover as large an area. Maps with smaller scales, like the two pictured here, can show a larger area but not as much detail.

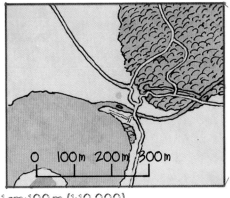

1 cm:100 m (1:10,000)

When 1 cm on the map represents 100 m, the pumpkin patch is no longer visible, but you can now see where it sits between the lake and forest.

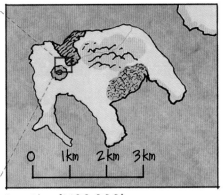

1 cm:1 km (1:100,000)

On this map, 1 cm stands for 1 km. At this scale, you can't see much detail, but you can see the outline of the whole island.

Pumpkin patch is 10m wide

Using a compass

It's picnic time! Can the mammoths find Picnic Paddock? When you want to work out which way to go, a compass is the tool you need. Its magnetic pointer shows which way is north—and once you find north, you can work out all the other directions, too.

Finding directions

A compass shows directions as angles, called bearings, measured clockwise from north (0°). The needle on a compass always points north, no matter which direction you point the compass in. To read a compass, line up the needle with the N for north marked on the dial.

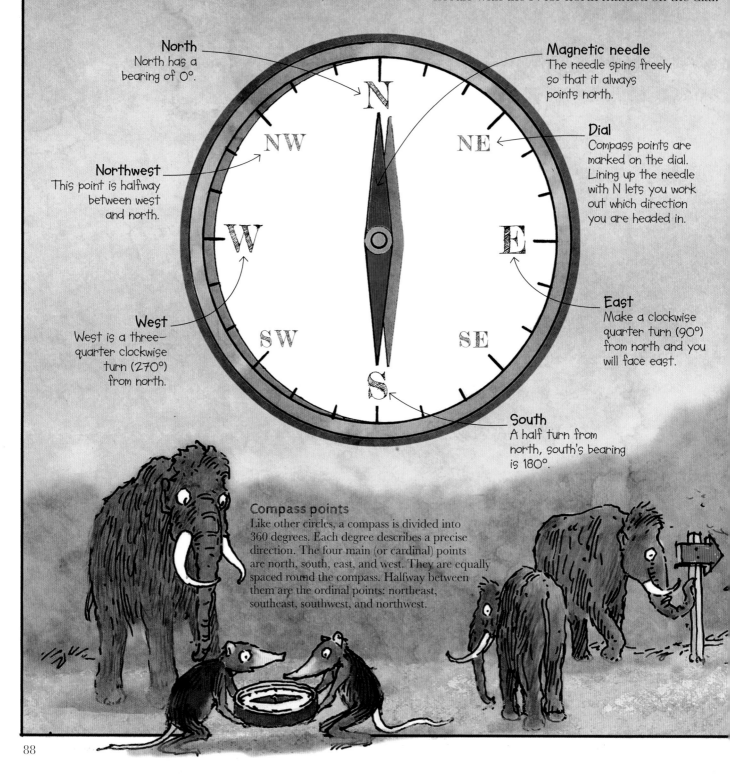

North
North has a bearing of 0°.

Magnetic needle
The needle spins freely so that it always points north.

Dial
Compass points are marked on the dial. Lining up the needle with N lets you work out which direction you are headed in.

Northwest
This point is halfway between west and north.

East
Make a clockwise quarter turn (90°) from north and you will face east.

West
West is a three-quarter clockwise turn (270°) from north.

South
A half turn from north, south's bearing is 180°.

Compass points
Like other circles, a compass is divided into 360 degrees. Each degree describes a precise direction. The four main (or cardinal) points are north, south, east, and west. They are equally spaced round the compass. Halfway between them are the ordinal points: northeast, southeast, southwest, and northwest.

Picnic Paddock

Pointing north
Maps have a north arrow.
Lining up the needle of a
compass with this arrow
lets you start working
out directions.

Step Three
From Rickety Bridge,
turn NORTHWEST
until you reach the
picnic spot.

Step Two
Now go EAST
and then cross
Rickety Bridge.

Step One
Go NORTH until
you reach the Old
Oak Tree.

Starting point

Directions to Picnic Paddock

Using the compass
You can use compass directions (bearings) to
navigate with a map. The mammoths are using
their compass skills to follow the instructions
and reach the picnic place.

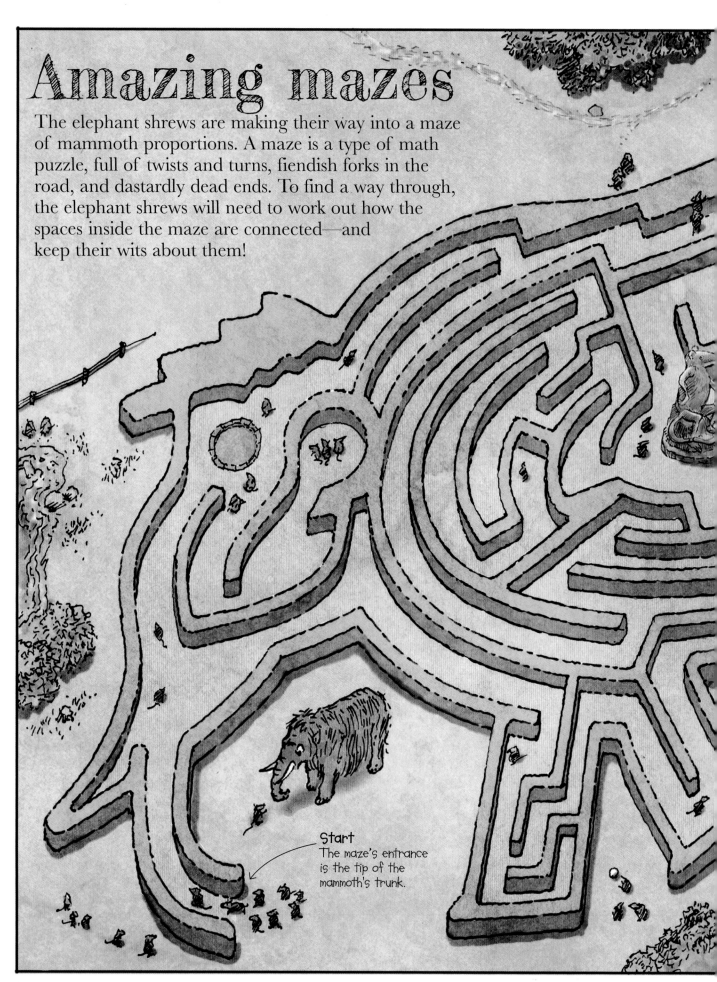

Amazing mazes

The elephant shrews are making their way into a maze of mammoth proportions. A maze is a type of math puzzle, full of twists and turns, fiendish forks in the road, and dastardly dead ends. To find a way through, the elephant shrews will need to work out how the spaces inside the maze are connected—and keep their wits about them!

Start
The maze's entrance is the tip of the mammoth's trunk.

Finish
The road to freedom is through the mammoth's tail.

Mammoth maze

Can you find a way through this magnificent maze? First make your way to the shrew statue in the center, then find the route to the exit. There is no secret formula—you need to use trial and error. It might help to remember the dead ends as you go, so you don't make the same mistake twice!

You can find the solution on page 160.

Which way now?
Mazes are much harder to solve from inside. The shrews could be stuck in there for hours!

Mazes and networks

To help you solve a maze, you can draw it as a network. This is a simple diagram that shows how parts of the maze connect to each other.

The right route
The diagram shows that when you get to point A you should head for point C, because B is a dead end.

Step 1
Mark each junction (where there is a choice of direction) and each dead end with a dot. Give each dot a letter. Finally, connect all the dots to show the different routes.

Step 2
Now write down the letters and connect them with straight lines, instead of the twists and turns of the maze itself. You will get a diagram that shows the quickest route from start to finish.

Start

End

Stupendous
shapes

Bamboozled builder

The elephant shrews are using lots of different lines in their bamboo building. The mammoth will need a long rest in the shade after carrying so many bamboo poles in the heat of the day.

Non-parallel

Non-parallel lines are not the same distance from each other all along their length. If the lines carried on, they would eventually meet.

Lines

Everyone knows what a line is—but in math, it's the word we use to describe something that joins two points. It can be straight or curved, and a straight line can point in any direction. The only thing you can measure on a line is its length. It doesn't have height or thickness.

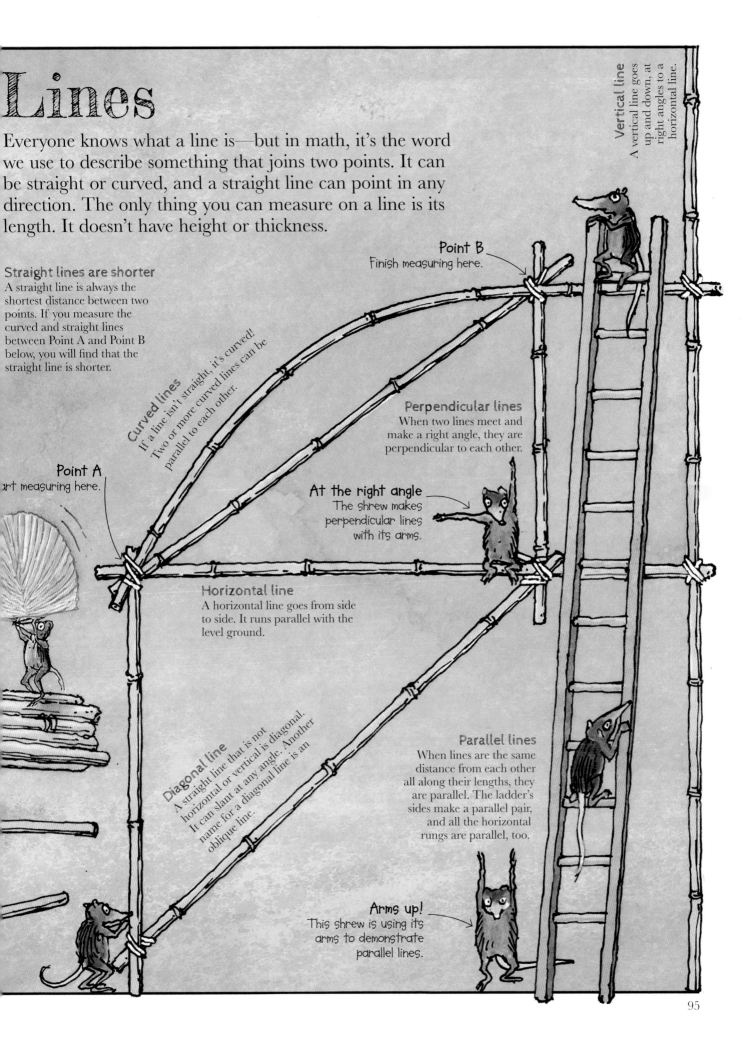

Straight lines are shorter
A straight line is always the shortest distance between two points. If you measure the curved and straight lines between Point A and Point B below, you will find that the straight line is shorter.

Curved lines
If a line isn't straight, it's curved! Two or more curved lines can be parallel to each other.

Point A
Start measuring here.

Point B
Finish measuring here.

Perpendicular lines
When two lines meet and make a right angle, they are perpendicular to each other.

At the right angle
The shrew makes perpendicular lines with its arms.

Horizontal line
A horizontal line goes from side to side. It runs parallel with the level ground.

Diagonal line
A straight line that is not horizontal or vertical is diagonal. It can slant at any angle. Another name for a diagonal line is an oblique line.

Parallel lines
When lines are the same distance from each other all along their lengths, they are parallel. The ladder's sides make a parallel pair, and all the horizontal rungs are parallel, too.

Arms up!
This shrew is using its arms to demonstrate parallel lines.

Regular polygons

In the regular room, all the polygons have equal-length sides and equal angles. There is only one way to make each regular polygon. Even when they change size they always remain the same polygon.

Regular pentagon
5 equal sides
5 equal angles

Regular decagon
10 equal sides
10 equal angles

Regular hexagon
6 equal sides
6 equal angles

Regular quadrilateral
4 equal sides
4 equal angles

Regular octagon
8 equal sides
8 equal angles

Number names
Polygons get their names from the Greek word for their number of angles. For example, pentagon means "five-angled."

Square
A regular quadrilateral is better known as a square.

2D shapes

Shapes that are flat are called 2D (short for two-dimensional) shapes. They have length and width but no thickness. 2D shapes can have straight sides or curved sides, or a mixture of both. Those with only straight edges belong to a group called the polygons. Here at the mammoth restaurant there are polygons all over the place.

Sides and angles
In every polygon, regular or irregular, the number of sides is the same as the number of angles.

Table for three?

At this popular dining spot, the table tops are all polygons—2D shapes with straight sides. The mammoths can choose to dine in the regular room, where all the tables are regular polygons, or in the irregular area. It's closer to the band, but the seating around the irregular tables can be a bit of a squeeze!

Equilateral triangle
A regular triangle is also known as an equilateral triangle.

Regular triangle
equal sides
equal angles

Not a polygon
A 2D shape with one or more curved edges is called a non-polygon.

Irregular polygons
The polygons in the bustling irregular room have sides of different lengths and angles that are not equal. There are lots of different ways of making each irregular polygon, as long as they have the right number of sides and angles.

KITCHEN

Irregular decagon
10 sides, not all equal
10 angles, not all equal

Irregular triangle
3 sides, not all equal
3 angles, not all equal

An irregular triangle is also called a scalene triangle

REGULAR ROOM

Irregular pentagon
5 sides, not all equal
5 angles, not all equal

Irregular hexagon
6 sides, not all equal
6 angles, not all equal

Irregular quadrilateral
4 sides, not all equal
4 angles, not all equal

Irregular octagon
8 sides, not all equal
8 angles, not all equal

IRREGULAR ROOM

Different shapes
Any shape with 8 sides and 8 angles that are not equal is an irregular octagon. This is just one example.

Equilateral triangle
This is the equality triangle. All three sides are the same length and all the angles are equal, too. This equilateral-triangle-shaped road sign is warning of trouble ahead.

Equal angles
These curved lines, called arcs, mark all the equal angles.

Equal sides
Double-dashes mark the sides of equal length.

Right-angled triangle
Two of the sides of this triangle are perpendicular, which means they make a right angle. The triangles that make up the bridge support are right-angled triangles.

Right angle (90°)

Triangles

A triangle is all about threes. It has three sides, three angles, and three vertices. It's a 2D shape with straight edges, so it's a polygon—and it has the smallest number of sides of all polygons. There are four main types of triangle, all seen here as the mammoth tiptoes across the triangle bridge.

Taking the strain
Triangles are the simplest and strongest shapes you can make from straight beams like these planks of wood.

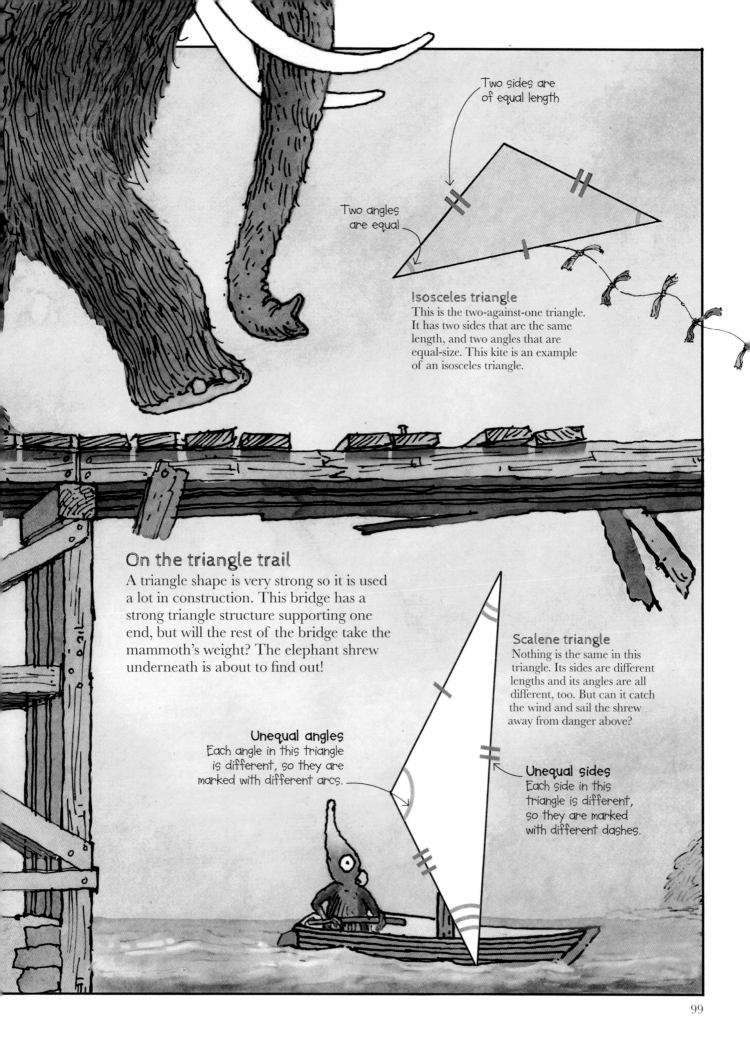

Two sides are
of equal length

Two angles
are equal

Isosceles triangle

This is the two-against-one triangle.
It has two sides that are the same
length, and two angles that are
equal-size. This kite is an example
of an isosceles triangle.

On the triangle trail

A triangle shape is very strong so it is used
a lot in construction. This bridge has a
strong triangle structure supporting one
end, but will the rest of the bridge take the
mammoth's weight? The elephant shrew
underneath is about to find out!

Scalene triangle

Nothing is the same in this
triangle. Its sides are different
lengths and its angles are all
different, too. But can it catch
the wind and sail the shrew
away from danger above?

Unequal angles
Each angle in this triangle
is different, so they are
marked with different arcs.

Unequal sides
Each side in this
triangle is different,
so they are marked
with different dashes.

Measuring a mammoth

Finding out the height of something tall can be tricky, but these elephant shrews have come up with a clever solution. All they need is a square of paper, a measuring tape, some triangle knowledge, and a very patient mammoth.

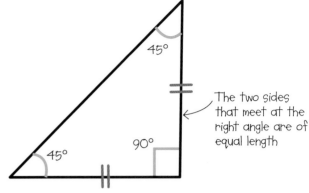

The two sides that meet at the right angle are of equal length

Triangle trick

How can the shrews measure the height of the mammoth without leaving the ground? By using a triangle! The shrews know that a right-angled triangle with two equal angles must have two sides the same length. By making a triangle using the mammoth's trunk, they can measure the distance of the side along the ground, and it will be the same as the distance to the top of the mammoth's head.

1. Make a measurer

The shrews take a paper square and fold it in half to make a triangle with one right angle and two identical 45° angles. Now they have a handy tool for finding 45° angles.

Each corner is 90°

Half of 90 is 45

2. Position the mammoth

Next the shrews politely ask the mammoth to extend its trunk. By positioning their paper triangle, they make a straight line from the ground to the top of the mammoth's head at a perfect 45° angle.

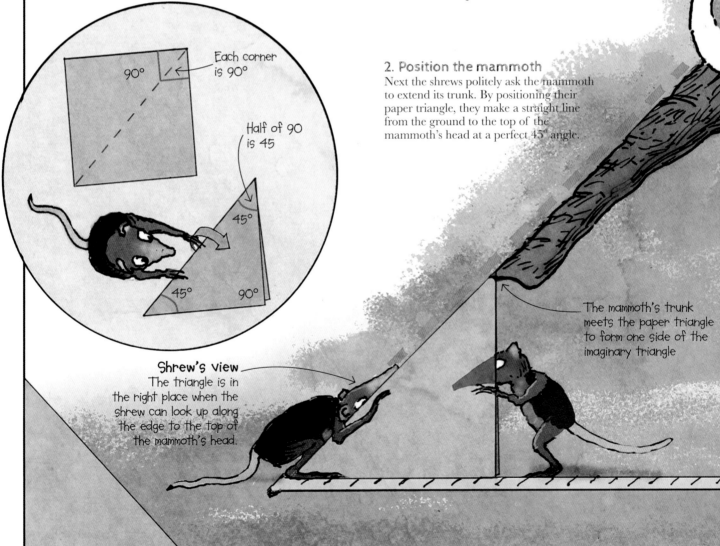

The mammoth's trunk meets the paper triangle to form one side of the imaginary triangle

Shrew's view
The triangle is in the right place when the shrew can look up along the edge to the top of the mammoth's head.

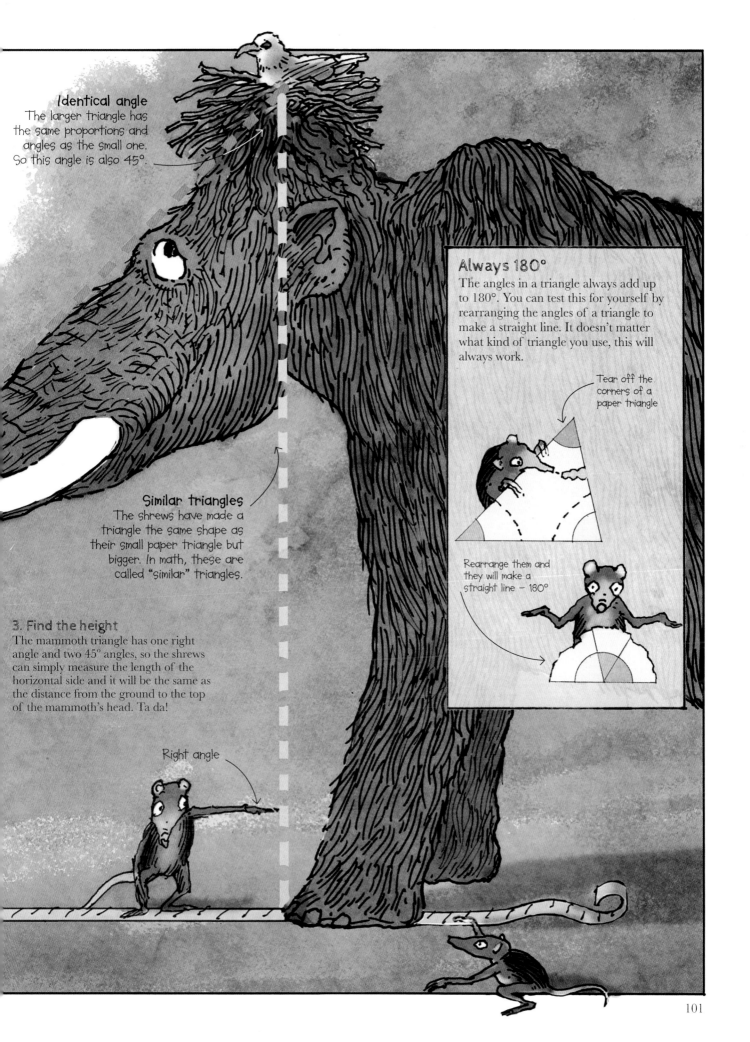

Identical angle
The larger triangle has the same proportions and angles as the small one. So this angle is also 45°.

Always 180°
The angles in a triangle always add up to 180°. You can test this for yourself by rearranging the angles of a triangle to make a straight line. It doesn't matter what kind of triangle you use, this will always work.

Tear off the corners of a paper triangle

Rearrange them and they will make a straight line – 180°

Similar triangles
The shrews have made a triangle the same shape as their small paper triangle but bigger. In math, these are called "similar" triangles.

3. Find the height
The mammoth triangle has one right angle and two 45° angles, so the shrews can simply measure the length of the horizontal side and it will be the same as the distance from the ground to the top of the mammoth's head. Ta da!

Right angle

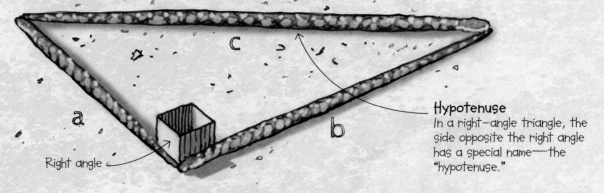

Hypotenuse
In a right-angle triangle, the side opposite the right angle has a special name—the "hypotenuse."

Right angle

Triangle test

In the warm afternoon sunshine, three snakes are stretched out enjoying a nice afternoon snooze. A passing mammoth and elephant shrew spot that the sleeping snakes have formed a right-angle triangle. They decide to test out one of the most famous math rules of all time: Pythagoras' Theorem.

Making squares

The rule says that if you form a square on each side of any right-angle triangle, the area of the biggest square will be the same as the area of the other two squares added together. Moving very quietly, the mammoth and shrew mark out a square next to each sleeping snake to put this theory to the test.

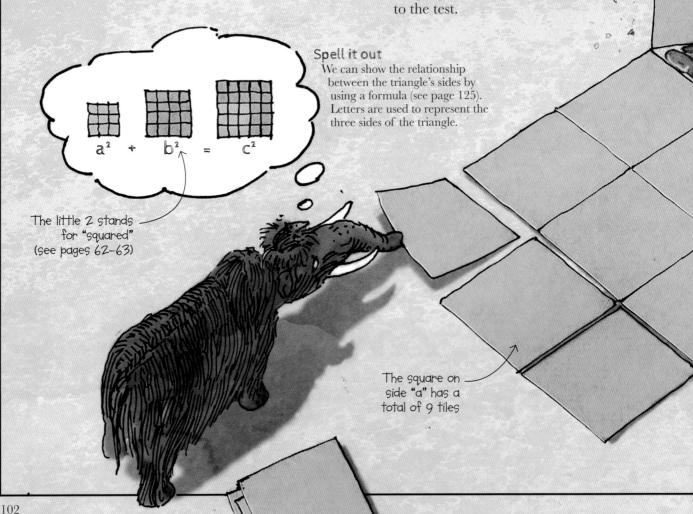

$$a^2 + b^2 = c^2$$

Spell it out
We can show the relationship between the triangle's sides by using a formula (see page 125). Letters are used to represent the three sides of the triangle.

The little 2 stands for "squared" (see pages 62–63)

The square on side "a" has a total of 9 tiles

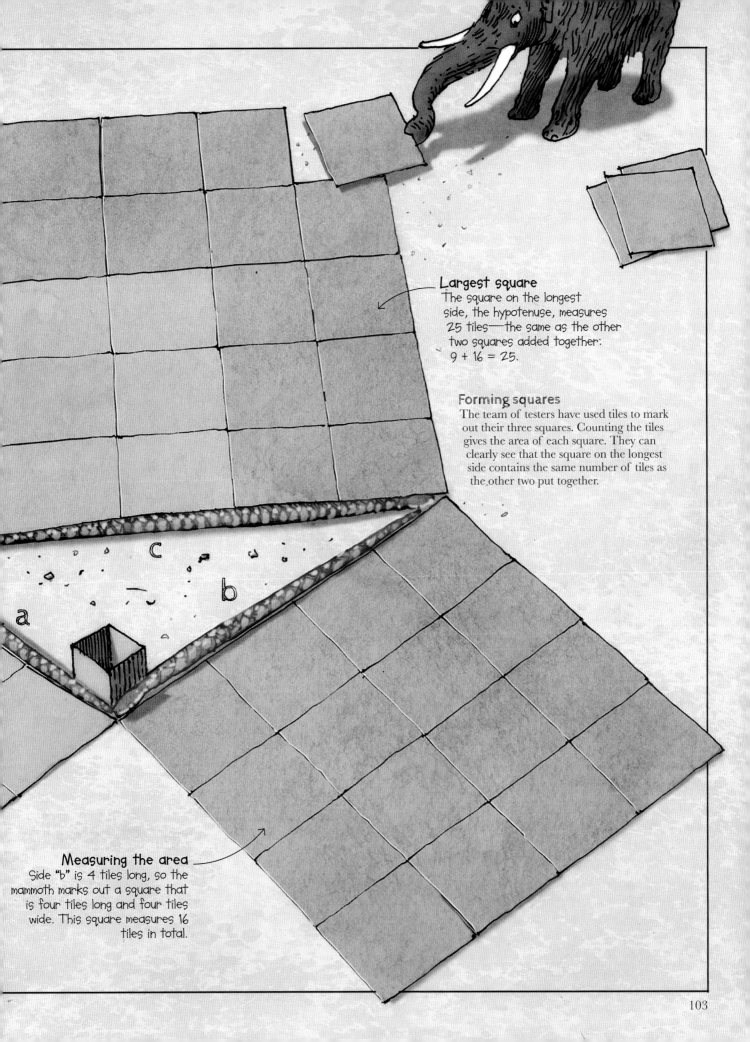

Largest square

The square on the longest side, the hypotenuse, measures 25 tiles—the same as the other two squares added together: $9 + 16 = 25$.

Forming squares

The team of testers have used tiles to mark out their three squares. Counting the tiles gives the area of each square. They can clearly see that the square on the longest side contains the same number of tiles as the other two put together.

c

b

a

Measuring the area

Side "b" is 4 tiles long, so the mammoth marks out a square that is four tiles long and four tiles wide. This square measures 16 tiles in total.

Quadrilaterals

A 2D polygon with four sides is called a quadrilateral. All quadrilaterals have four sides, four angles, and four vertices. Like all polygons, quadrilaterals can be regular, with equal sides and angles, or irregular, with sides and angles that are different from each other.

Name that shape!

All these shapes are members of the quadrilateral family. All the shapes below are parallelograms, while the ones on the facing page are not.

Sides that are parallel are marked with matching arrow symbols

Dashes denote that the opposite sides are of equal length

Parallelogram
The clue is in the name! A parallelogram has two sets of parallel sides. Its opposite sides are the same length and its opposite angles are equal, too.

Angles that are equal are marked with arcs

Rectangle
A rectangle has opposite sides of equal length. These opposite sides are parallel so that makes it a parallelogram. But it's a special type of parallelogram, because all four angles are equal (and they are all right angles).

Right angles
Each of the rectangle's four angles is 90°.

Square
A square is a special rectangle that is also a parallelogram, because it has two sets of parallel sides. What makes it unique is that all four sides are the same length and all four angles are equal.

Rhombus
This quadrilateral is part of the parallelogram club but not in the rectangle gang. Its opposite sides are parallel and its opposite angles are equal, but they aren't right angles. All four of its sides are equal in length.

Kite

A kite shape has two sets of equal-length sides. The equal sides are adjacent, which means they meet at a vertex. A kite's opposite angles are equal.

This angle and the one opposite are equal

A kite shape has two adjacent long sides of equal length and two shorter ones that are also equal

Awesome foursome

"Quad" means "four" in Latin. Things that start with "quad–," such as "quadrilateral" or "quad bike," always have four of something!

Two triangles

The angles inside a quadrilateral always add up to 360°. You can prove this is true by using the triangle test. Any quadrilateral, no matter its size or shape, can be split into two triangles. A triangle's angles always add up to 180°. That means that the quadrilateral's angles must be 2 x 180°—which equals 360°.

Trapezium

A trapezium is also called a trapezoid. It has one pair of parallel sides. If the two non-parallel sides are the same length, as with this shape, it gets to call itself an isosceles trapezium.

A right-angled trapezium has two right angles and one pair of parallel sides

Irregular quadrilateral

This quadrilateral has no parallel sides, no equal angles, and all its edges are different lengths. It is an irregular quadrilateral. Back to the drawing board!

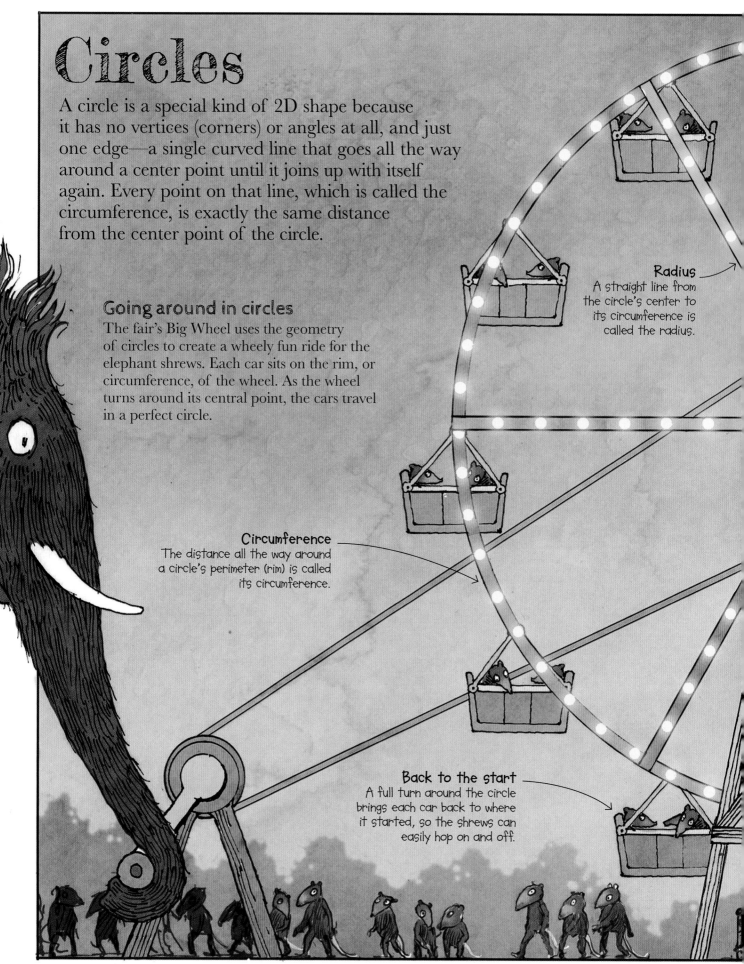

Circles

A circle is a special kind of 2D shape because it has no vertices (corners) or angles at all, and just one edge—a single curved line that goes all the way around a center point until it joins up with itself again. Every point on that line, which is called the circumference, is exactly the same distance from the center point of the circle.

Going around in circles

The fair's Big Wheel uses the geometry of circles to create a wheely fun ride for the elephant shrews. Each car sits on the rim, or circumference, of the wheel. As the wheel turns around its central point, the cars travel in a perfect circle.

Radius
A straight line from the circle's center to its circumference is called the radius.

Circumference
The distance all the way around a circle's perimeter (rim) is called its circumference.

Back to the start
A full turn around the circle brings each car back to where it started, so the shrews can easily hop on and off.

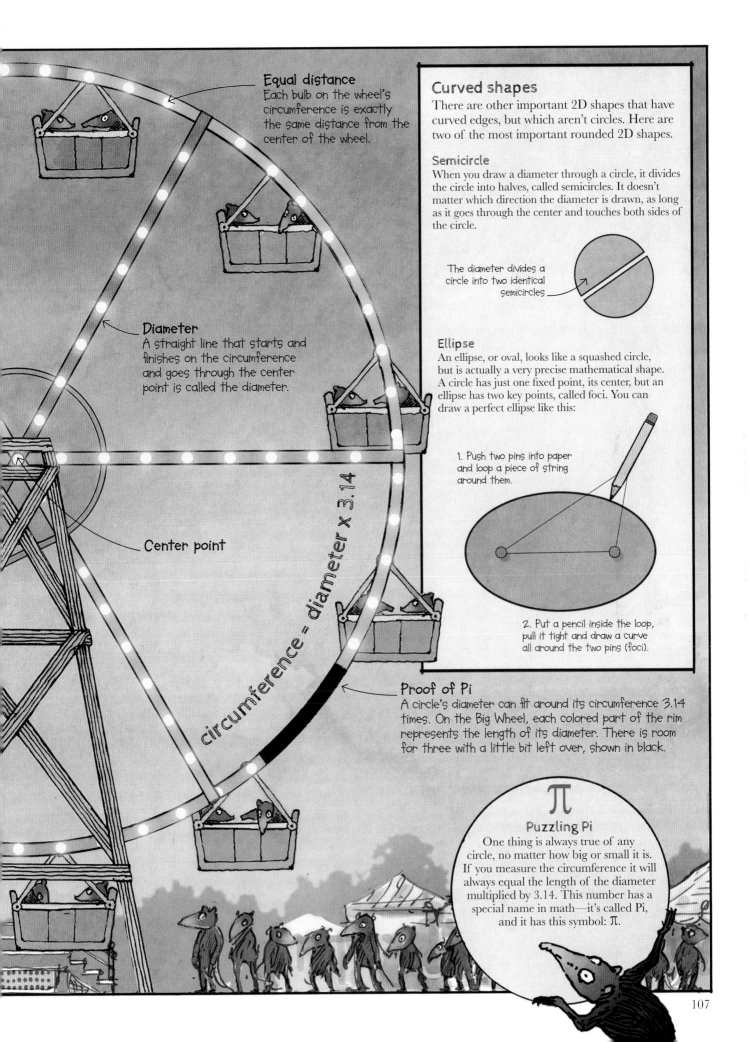

Equal distance
Each bulb on the wheel's circumference is exactly the same distance from the center of the wheel.

Diameter
A straight line that starts and finishes on the circumference and goes through the center point is called the diameter.

Center point

circumference = diameter x 3.14

Curved shapes
There are other important 2D shapes that have curved edges, but which aren't circles. Here are two of the most important rounded 2D shapes.

Semicircle
When you draw a diameter through a circle, it divides the circle into halves, called semicircles. It doesn't matter which direction the diameter is drawn, as long as it goes through the center and touches both sides of the circle.

The diameter divides a circle into two identical semicircles

Ellipse
An ellipse, or oval, looks like a squashed circle, but is actually a very precise mathematical shape. A circle has just one fixed point, its center, but an ellipse has two key points, called foci. You can draw a perfect ellipse like this:

1. Push two pins into paper and loop a piece of string around them.

2. Put a pencil inside the loop, pull it tight and draw a curve all around the two pins (foci).

Proof of Pi
A circle's diameter can fit around its circumference 3.14 times. On the Big Wheel, each colored part of the rim represents the length of its diameter. There is room for three with a little bit left over, shown in black.

π
Puzzling Pi
One thing is always true of any circle, no matter how big or small it is. If you measure the circumference it will always equal the length of the diameter multiplied by 3.14. This number has a special name in math—it's called Pi, and it has this symbol: π.

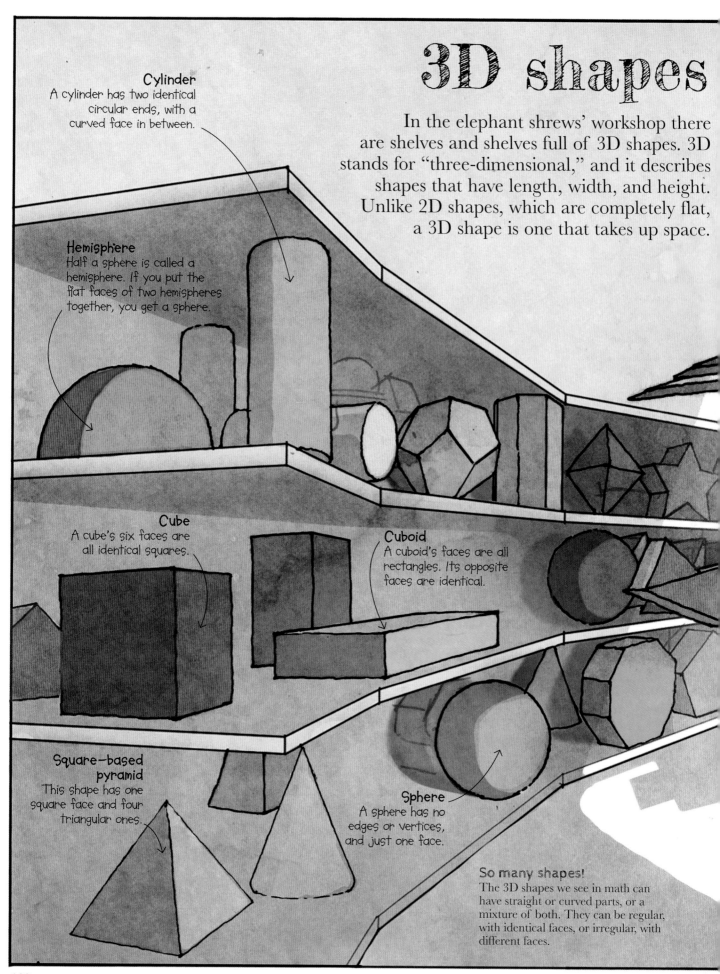

3D shapes

In the elephant shrews' workshop there are shelves and shelves full of 3D shapes. 3D stands for "three-dimensional," and it describes shapes that have length, width, and height. Unlike 2D shapes, which are completely flat, a 3D shape is one that takes up space.

Cylinder
A cylinder has two identical circular ends, with a curved face in between.

Hemisphere
Half a sphere is called a hemisphere. If you put the flat faces of two hemispheres together, you get a sphere.

Cube
A cube's six faces are all identical squares.

Cuboid
A cuboid's faces are all rectangles. Its opposite faces are identical.

Square-based pyramid
This shape has one square face and four triangular ones.

Sphere
A sphere has no edges or vertices, and just one face.

So many shapes!
The 3D shapes we see in math can have straight or curved parts, or a mixture of both. They can be regular, with identical faces, or irregular, with different faces.

Polly-what?
Any 3D shape whose faces are all polygons is called a polyhedron (say "polly-hee-dron").

Different faces
3D shapes with faces of different sizes and shapes are irregular. How many irregular 3D shapes can you spot in the mammoth model? (Answer on page 160.)

Face
The surface of a 3D object is a face. It can be flat or curved.

Edge
An edge is the line where two or more faces of a 3D shape meet.

Vertex
A vertex is a corner. It's where two or more edges of the shape meet.

Mammoth model

The elephant shrews are busy building a magnificent 3D mammoth model. 3D objects come in all different shapes and sizes. The shrews are using geometric shapes (the ones we see in math), but any object that takes up space is a 3D shape. You are a 3D shape and so are the pages of this book!

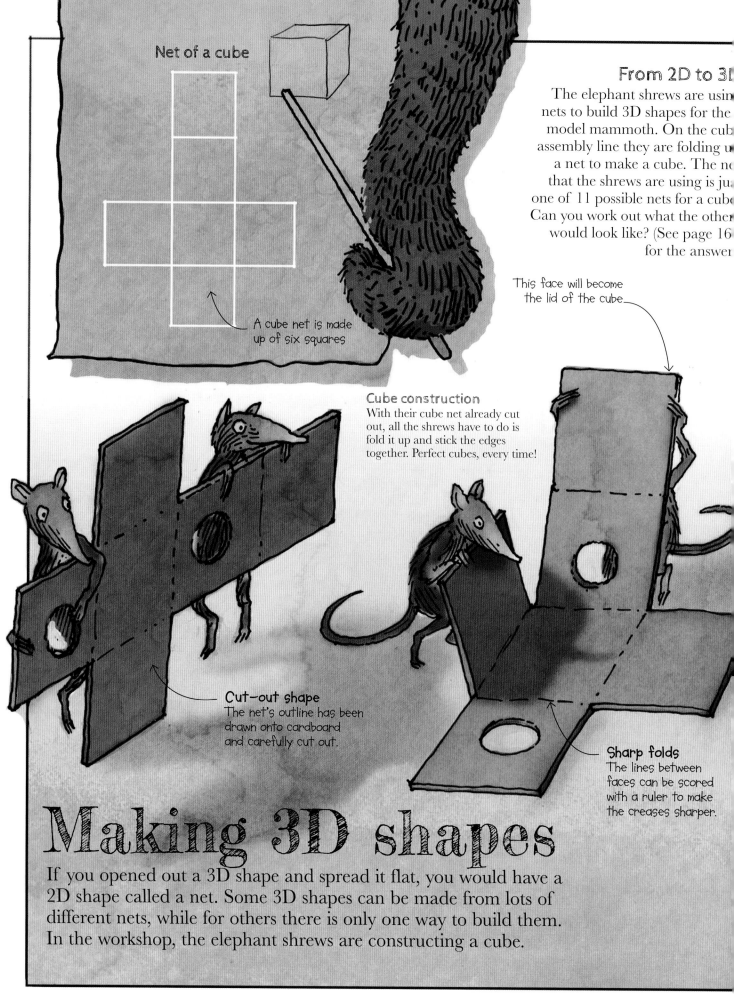

Net of a cube

A cube net is made
up of six squares

From 2D to 3D

The elephant shrews are using
nets to build 3D shapes for the
model mammoth. On the cube
assembly line they are folding up
a net to make a cube. The net
that the shrews are using is just
one of 11 possible nets for a cube.
Can you work out what the others
would look like? (See page 16...
for the answer.)

This face will become
the lid of the cube

Cube construction
With their cube net already cut
out, all the shrews have to do is
fold it up and stick the edges
together. Perfect cubes, every time!

Cut-out shape
The net's outline has been
drawn onto cardboard
and carefully cut out.

Sharp folds
The lines between
faces can be scored
with a ruler to make
the creases sharper.

Making 3D shapes

If you opened out a 3D shape and spread it flat, you would have a
2D shape called a net. Some 3D shapes can be made from lots of
different nets, while for others there is only one way to build them.
In the workshop, the elephant shrews are constructing a cube.

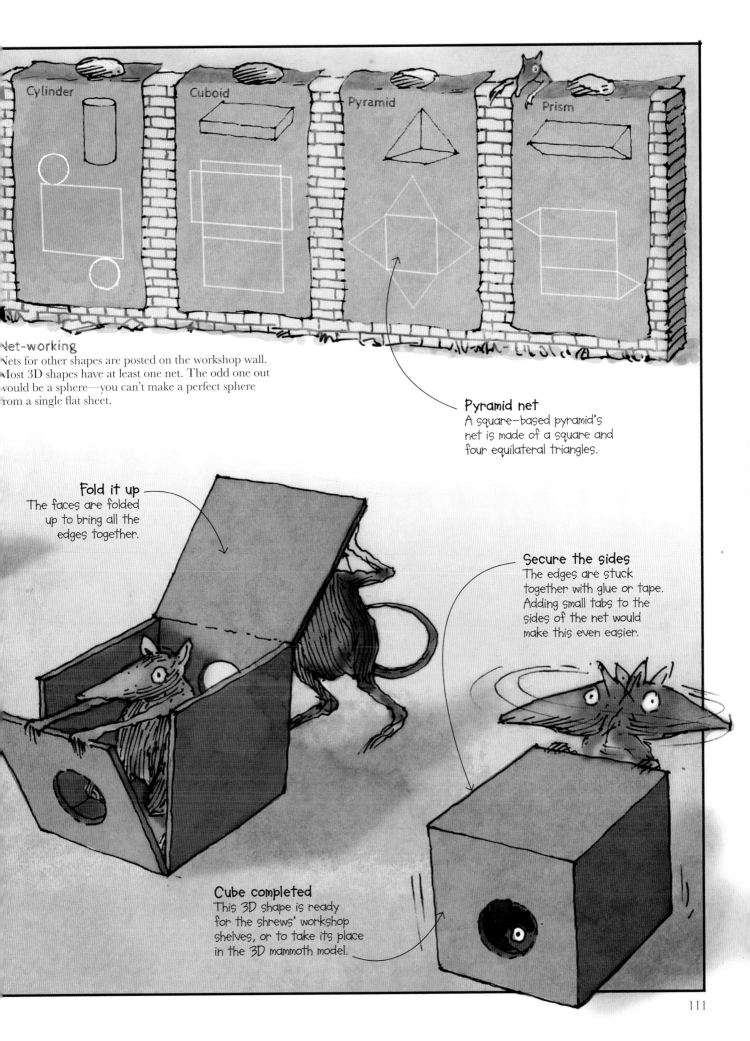

Cylinder

Cuboid

Pyramid

Prism

Net-working

Nets for other shapes are posted on the workshop wall.
Most 3D shapes have at least one net. The odd one out
would be a sphere—you can't make a perfect sphere
from a single flat sheet.

Pyramid net
A square-based pyramid's
net is made of a square and
four equilateral triangles.

Fold it up
The faces are folded
up to bring all the
edges together.

Secure the sides
The edges are stuck
together with glue or tape.
Adding small tabs to the
sides of the net would
make this even easier.

Cube completed
This 3D shape is ready
for the shrews' workshop
shelves, or to take its place
in the 3D mammoth model.

Polyhedrons

A polyhedron is a 3D shape with flat faces (made from polygons) and edges that are straight. Like most shapes in math, they can be regular, with faces that are regular polygons of the same size, or irregular, where the faces are polygons of different sizes and shapes.

Octagonal prism
This shape's parallel ends are octagons—eight-sided polygons.

Rectangular prism
Also called a cuboid prism, its opposite ends are rectangles.

Triangular prism
This wedge of cheese has ends that are triangles.

Prism treats

At tea-time in the workshop, the elephant shrews are tucking into a range of snacks that have something in common—all except one of them are prism-shaped. A prism is a special kind of polyhedron—its ends are the same size and shape, and parallel to each other. This means that a prism is the same size and shape all along its length.

Regular polyhedrons

A 3D shape whose faces are all identical regular polygons is called a regular polyhedron. Amazingly, out of all the 3D shapes in the world, there are only five shapes in this exclusive club—and three of them are made from the same shape—the equilateral triangle.

Tetrahedron
4 faces
4 vertices
6 edges
— Faces are equilateral triangles

Cube
6 faces
8 vertices
12 edges
— Faces are squares

Octahedron
8 faces
6 vertices
12 edges
— Faces are equilateral triangles

Dodecahedron
12 faces
20 vertices
30 edges
— Faces are pentagons

Icosahedron
20 faces
12 vertices
30 edges
— Faces are equilateral triangles

Is it a prism?
A cylinder has two identical, parallel ends. But it has curved edges, so although this Swiss roll is a tasty snack, it can't be a prism.

Sugar cube
A cube, made from square faces, is the only prism that's also a regular polyhedron.

Slicing a prism
If you cut through a prism parallel to one of its ends, the new face will be the same size and shape as the original face.

Impossible shapes

Impossible shapes are those that can be drawn, but couldn't be constructed in real life. They are optical illusions that work because your brain is programmed to make sense of the information it receives from your eyes. Here are some examples of 2D images that trick the brain into seeing impossible 3D objects.

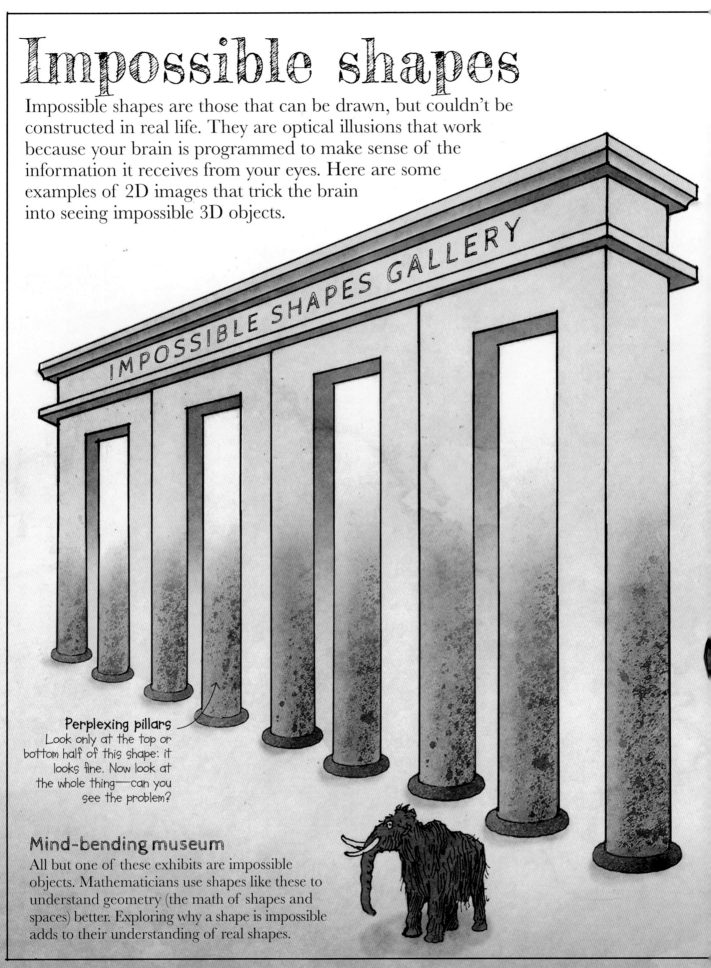

IMPOSSIBLE SHAPES GALLERY

Perplexing pillars
Look only at the top or bottom half of this shape: it looks fine. Now look at the whole thing—can you see the problem?

Mind-bending museum
All but one of these exhibits are impossible objects. Mathematicians use shapes like these to understand geometry (the math of shapes and spaces) better. Exploring why a shape is impossible adds to their understanding of real shapes.

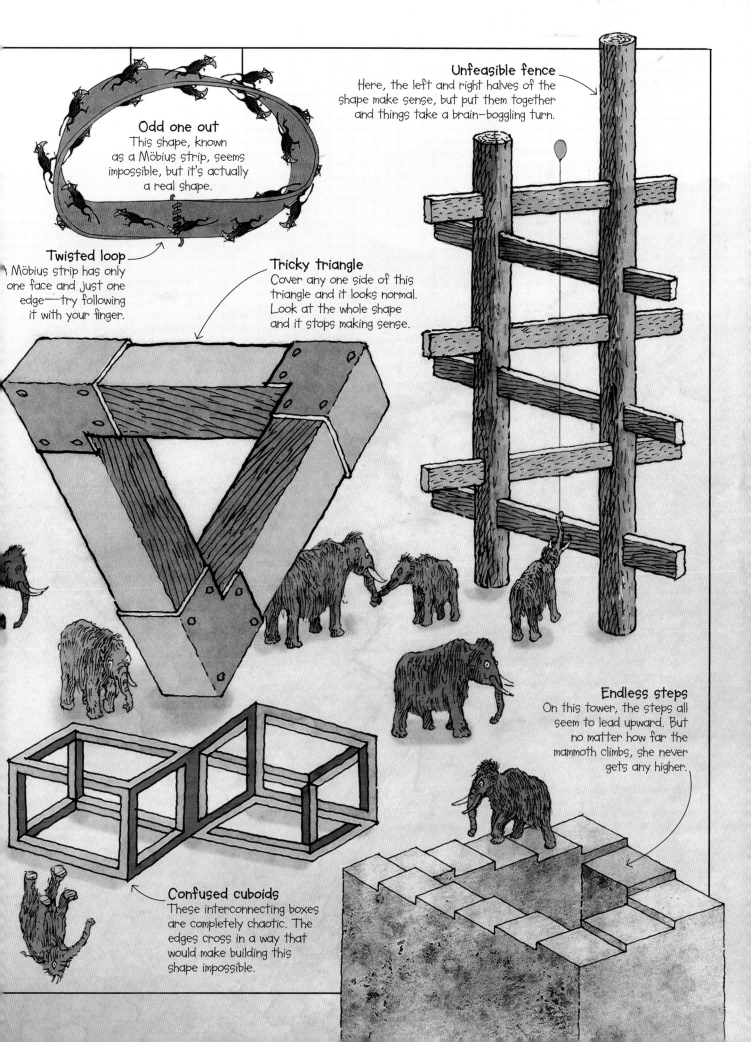

Odd one out
This shape, known as a Möbius strip, seems impossible, but it's actually a real shape.

Unfeasible fence
Here, the left and right halves of the shape make sense, but put them together and things take a brain-boggling turn.

Twisted loop
A Möbius strip has only one face and just one edge—try following it with your finger.

Tricky triangle
Cover any one side of this triangle and it looks normal. Look at the whole shape and it stops making sense.

Endless steps
On this tower, the steps all seem to lead upward. But no matter how far the mammoth climbs, she never gets any higher.

Confused cuboids
These interconnecting boxes are completely chaotic. The edges cross in a way that would make building this shape impossible.

How much?
How big?
How long?

Measuring up

The mammoth sculptor is getting ready to carve a statue. First, this oversized artist must find a block of stone with exactly the right dimensions. The elephant shrews are hard at work measuring the width, length, and height of a block. Will this be the block that becomes the mammoth's next masterpiece?

Length

The distance between two points is called length. Length can be measured using units such as miles, inches, kilometers, meters, centimeters, and millimeters. Width, height, and depth are all just different words for the same thing—length.

Measuring tiny things

To measure small things, you need to use small units of measurement. There are 10 mm in 1 cm, and 100 cm in 1 m. This ant is only 8 mm long. If you measured it in meters it would be 0.008 m—how confusing!

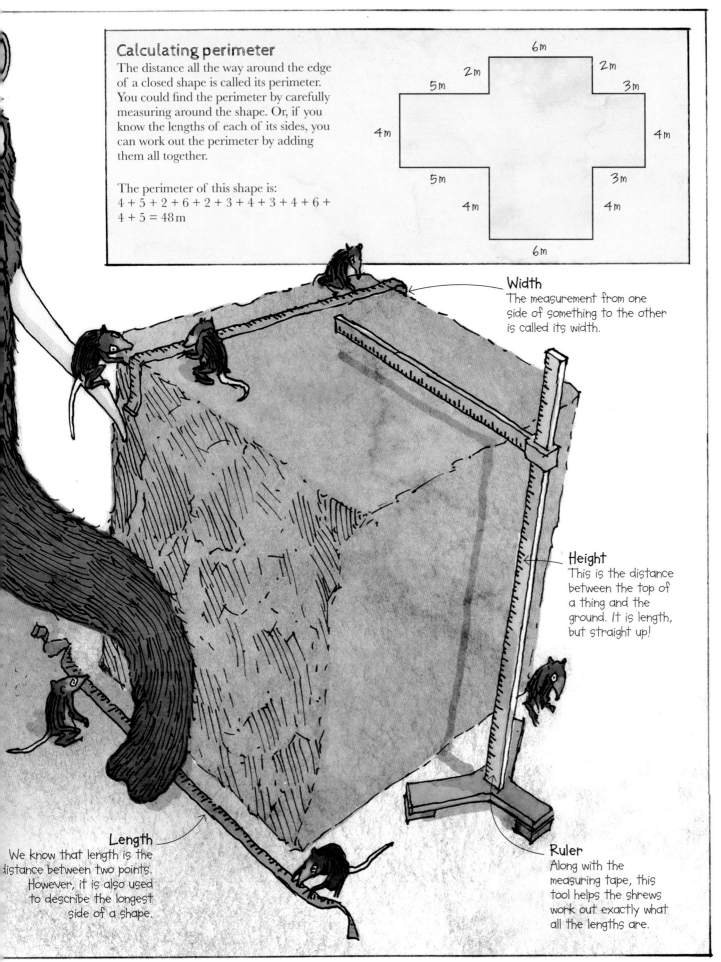

Calculating perimeter

The distance all the way around the edge of a closed shape is called its perimeter. You could find the perimeter by carefully measuring around the shape. Or, if you know the lengths of each of its sides, you can work out the perimeter by adding them all together.

The perimeter of this shape is:
$$4 + 5 + 2 + 6 + 2 + 3 + 4 + 3 + 4 + 6 + 4 + 5 = 48\,m$$

6 m
2 m
2 m
5 m
3 m
4 m
4 m
5 m
3 m
4 m
4 m
6 m

Width
The measurement from one side of something to the other is called its width.

Height
This is the distance between the top of a thing and the ground. It is length, but straight up!

Length
We know that length is the distance between two points. However, it is also used to describe the longest side of a shape.

Ruler
Along with the measuring tape, this tool helps the shrews work out exactly what all the lengths are.

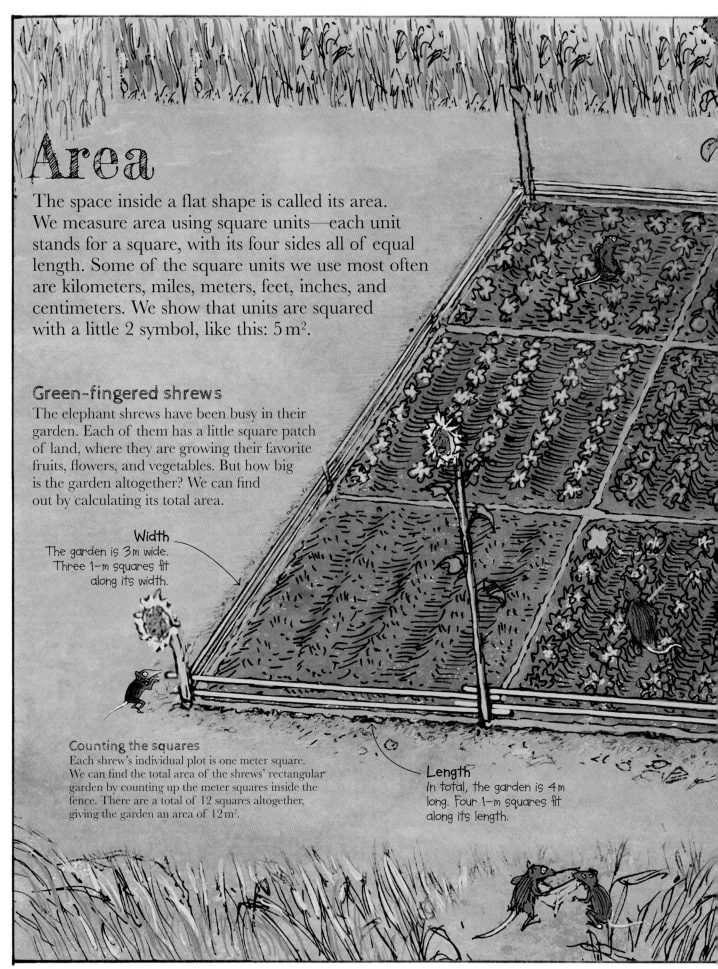

Area

The space inside a flat shape is called its area. We measure area using square units—each unit stands for a square, with its four sides all of equal length. Some of the square units we use most often are kilometers, miles, meters, feet, inches, and centimeters. We show that units are squared with a little 2 symbol, like this: $5\,m^2$.

Green-fingered shrews

The elephant shrews have been busy in their garden. Each of them has a little square patch of land, where they are growing their favorite fruits, flowers, and vegetables. But how big is the garden altogether? We can find out by calculating its total area.

Width
The garden is 3m wide. Three 1-m squares fit along its width.

Counting the squares
Each shrew's individual plot is one meter square. We can find the total area of the shrews' rectangular garden by counting up the meter squares inside the fence. There are a total of 12 squares altogether, giving the garden an area of $12\,m^2$.

Length
In total, the garden is 4m long. Four 1-m squares fit along its length.

Unit square
Each shrew's patch of garden is a square 1m long and 1m across. So the area of each square is 1 square meter, or 1m².

Work it out
Another way of finding the area of a rectangle is to multiply the length by the width. Here, the garden is 4m long by 3m wide. 4 x 3 = 12, so the area is 12m².

area = length x width

Sweet, sweet volume

What is the volume of this box? The elephant shrews are eager to find out. To aid them in their quest, they have whittled hundreds of sugar lumps into perfect cubes. With the mammoth's help, they are filling the box with tidy rows of sugar.

Volume

Volume is the amount of space a 3D object takes up. It is a way of describing how big something is in three dimensions. Volume is measured using cubic units—each unit represents a cube, with its height, width, and length all one unit long. We show cubic units with a little 3, like this: $4\,m^3$.

A perfect cube

The shrews have carefully measured every sugar lump. Each piece of sugar is a perfect cube, with each of its sides measuring 1 cm. That gives each cube a volume of $1\,cm^3$.

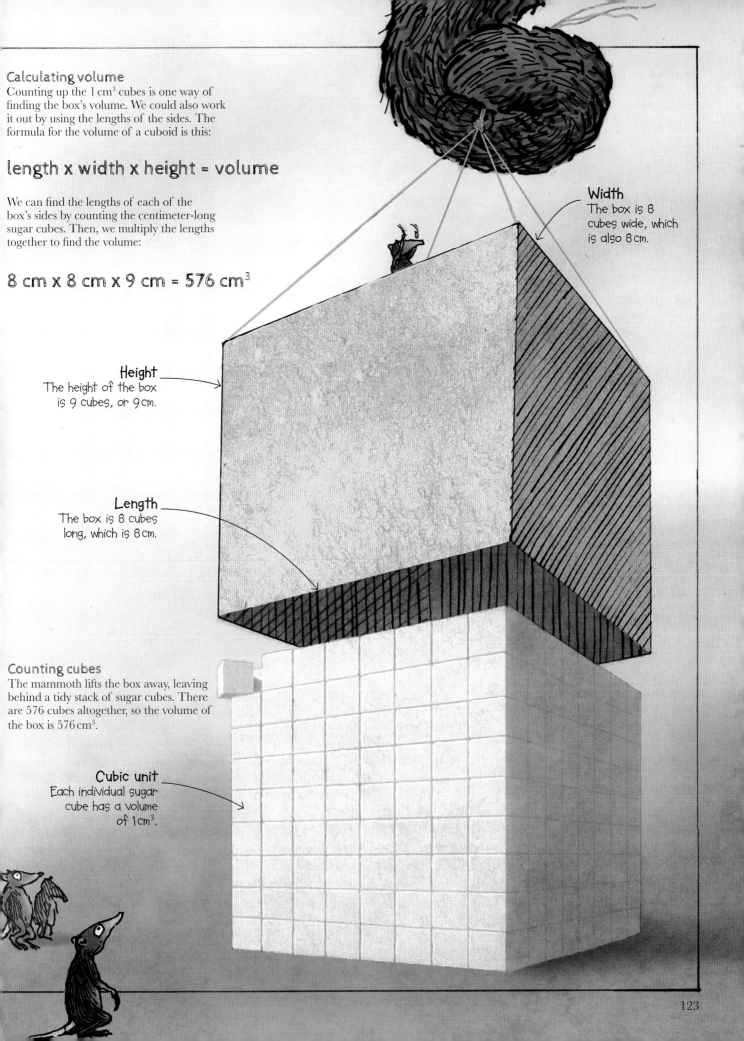

Calculating volume

Counting up the 1 cm³ cubes is one way of finding the box's volume. We could also work it out by using the lengths of the sides. The formula for the volume of a cuboid is this:

length x width x height = volume

We can find the lengths of each of the box's sides by counting the centimeter-long sugar cubes. Then, we multiply the lengths together to find the volume:

8 cm x 8 cm x 9 cm = 576 cm³

Width
The box is 8 cubes wide, which is also 8 cm.

Height
The height of the box is 9 cubes, or 9 cm.

Length
The box is 8 cubes long, which is 8 cm.

Counting cubes

The mammoth lifts the box away, leaving behind a tidy stack of sugar cubes. There are 576 cubes altogether, so the volume of the box is 576 cm³.

Cubic unit
Each individual sugar cube has a volume of 1 cm³.

Speed

To measure speed, you need to know two different things: how far something has traveled, and how long it took to get there. Once you know these, you can work out how fast an object was going. Speed is a compound unit of measurement, which means that it involves two or more different measurements.

Charging mammoth
The mammoth thunders down the track—but how fast is this speed demon actually moving?

Whoa nelly!
The shrew rider will have to hold on tight. A mammoth moving at top speed may take a while to slow down.

100 m

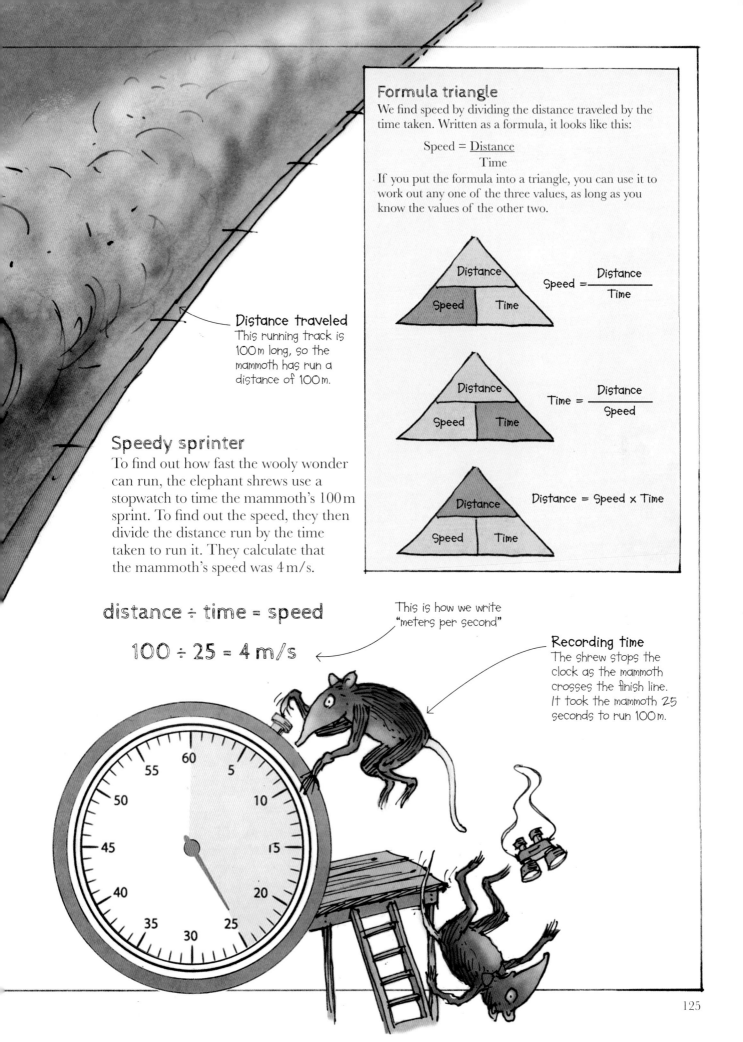

Formula triangle

We find speed by dividing the distance traveled by the time taken. Written as a formula, it looks like this:

$$Speed = \frac{Distance}{Time}$$

If you put the formula into a triangle, you can use it to work out any one of the three values, as long as you know the values of the other two.

$$Speed = \frac{Distance}{Time}$$

$$Time = \frac{Distance}{Speed}$$

$$Distance = Speed \times Time$$

Distance traveled
This running track is 100 m long, so the mammoth has run a distance of 100 m.

Speedy sprinter

To find out how fast the wooly wonder can run, the elephant shrews use a stopwatch to time the mammoth's 100 m sprint. To find out the speed, they then divide the distance run by the time taken to run it. They calculate that the mammoth's speed was 4 m/s.

distance ÷ time = speed

100 ÷ 25 = 4 m/s

This is how we write "meters per second"

Recording time
The shrew stops the clock as the mammoth crosses the finish line. It took the mammoth 25 seconds to run 100 m.

Weight and mass

The amount of matter or material inside an object is called its mass. People often say weight when they mean mass, but weight is something different—it's the amount of gravity acting on an object and is measured in newtons (N). Mass is measured in metric units such as milligrams, grams, kilograms, and metric tons.

Measuring mass

Now the elephant shrews know what mass is, they're eager to measure themselves. They've roped the mammoth in, too, as well as some other friends. Each animal will be measured using the metric units best suited to its size.

Tiny ant
The ant waits patiently while the shrew reads the scales. Its mass is tiny—only 5 mg.

Small shrew
One shrew stands on the scales while another notes down its mass, 10 g.

5 mg

10 g

Milligrams
We measure the mass of tiny, light things using tiny units—milligrams (mg). There are even tinier units, such as nanograms, but they are used to measure the mass of objects so small that you can only see them with a microscope.

Grams
There are 1,000 mg in each gram (g). A paperclip has a mass of around 1 g, a banana is around 30 g, and a paperback book around 140 g.

15 kg

Kilograms
There are 1,000 g in 1 kilogram (kg).
A liter bottle of water has a mass of
around 1 kg. A pet cat is around 4 kg,
and a grand piano can be up to 500 kg.

Mega mammoth
The mammoth is the
largest animal here,
weighing in at an
impressive 6
metric tons.

Weighty snake
A large snake rests on this
weighing scale. From a safe
distance, a shrew takes a
careful look at the snake's
mass—15 kg.

6 metric tons

Metric tons
Very heavy things can be measured using
tons. Each metric ton is equivalent to
1,000 kg. A walrus has a mass of around
1 metric ton, an African elephant is about
4 metric tons, and a semi truck is around
40 metric tons.

Telling time

Measuring the passing of time helps us keep track of things. You might want to know how long a cake will take to bake, how long a journey will last, or when to meet up with your friends. Seconds, minutes, and hours are the units we use to measure time across the course of a day. To tell the time, you need a clock.

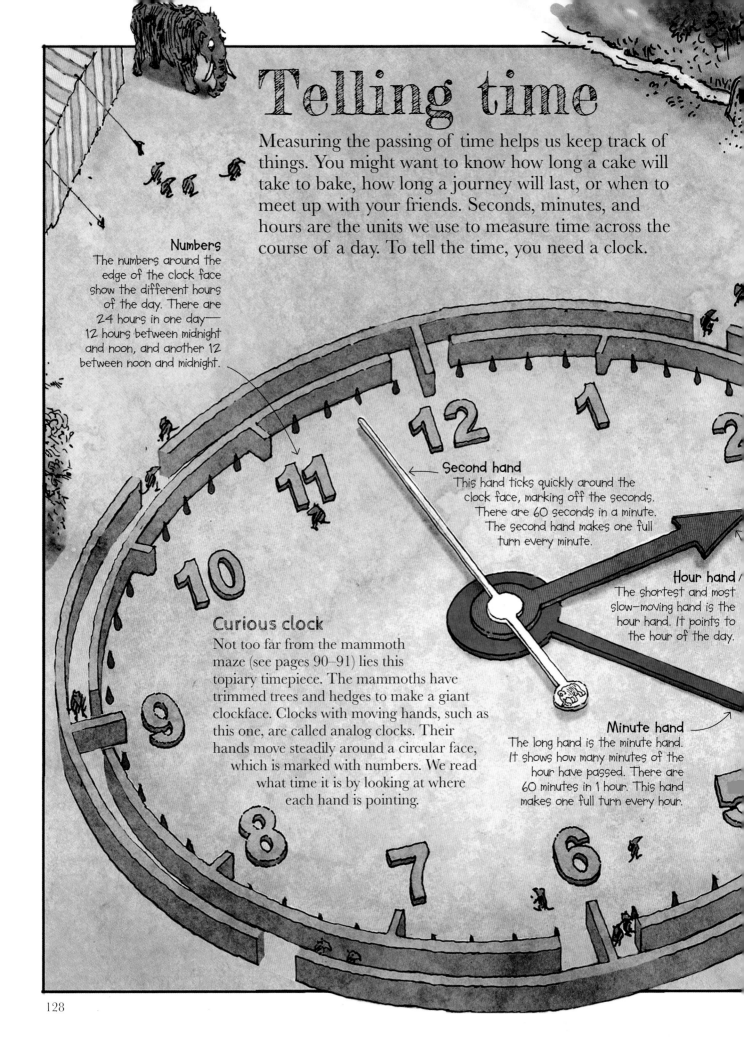

Numbers

The numbers around the edge of the clock face show the different hours of the day. There are 24 hours in one day— 12 hours between midnight and noon, and another 12 between noon and midnight.

Second hand

This hand ticks quickly around the clock face, marking off the seconds. There are 60 seconds in a minute. The second hand makes one full turn every minute.

Hour hand

The shortest and most slow-moving hand is the hour hand. It points to the hour of the day.

Curious clock

Not too far from the mammoth maze (see pages 90–91) lies this topiary timepiece. The mammoths have trimmed trees and hedges to make a giant clockface. Clocks with moving hands, such as this one, are called analog clocks. Their hands move steadily around a circular face, which is marked with numbers. We read what time it is by looking at where each hand is pointing.

Minute hand

The long hand is the minute hand. It shows how many minutes of the hour have passed. There are 60 minutes in 1 hour. This hand makes one full turn every hour.

Using digital clocks

Digital clocks show the time using two numbers. The first number shows the hour of the day, and the second the number of minutes past that hour. Some digital clocks use the 12-hour clock, with the letters "am" and "pm" showing whether it is morning (am) or afternoon (pm). Others use the 24-hour clock, which starts at 00.00 for midnight and counts the 24 hours until the following midnight.

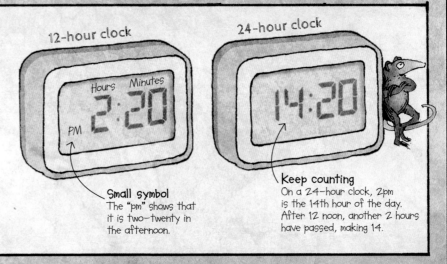

12-hour clock

Hours Minutes

PM

Small symbol
The "pm" shows that it is two-twenty in the afternoon.

24-hour clock

Keep counting
On a 24-hour clock, 2pm is the 14th hour of the day. After 12 noon, another 2 hours have passed, making 14.

Minute marks
The small marks without numbers show the 60 minutes each hour is broken into. We can count these in groups of 5, between each of the large numbers on the clock face.

Clockwise
All of the clock's hands move in this direction, which is called "clockwise."

On the hour
The time is "on the hour" when the minute hand is pointing up to the 12. We say "o'clock"—this is 8 o'clock.

Half past
It is halfway through an hour when the minute hand points to the 6. This clock is showing half past two, or "two thirty."

Minutes past
Before the minute hand reaches the 6, we count the number of minutes past the hour. This is 5 past 4, or "four oh five."

Quarter after
We say it is quarter after an hour when the minute hand points to the 3. The time on this clock is quarter after ten.

Minutes to
Once the minute hand has passed the 6, we look at the number of minutes left until the next hour. This is 25 to 5, or "four thirty-five."

Quarter to
When the minute hand points to the 9, the time is quarter to the next hour. This clock is showing quarter to seven.

Temperature

Sometimes you need to know exactly how hot or cold something is. By measuring temperature, you can compare today's weather to yesterday's, make sure your fridge is keeping food cool and fresh, or check your own temperature to find out if you're fighting fit or feverish.

Different scales
This thermometer measures temperature in two different units: degrees Celsius (°C) and degrees Fahrenheit (°F).

Read the scales
The markings on either side of the thermometer are the scales. Similar to a ruler or a number line, the scale tells you how high or low the temperature is.

Weather watching
A simple thermometer contains a colored liquid that expands when it is hot and contracts when it is cold, which makes it move up or down the tube. The scale on the side means that we can read the temperature in degrees.

What a scorcher!
The hotter it gets, the higher the liquid in the thermometer rises. A temperature of 108°F (42°C) means the mammoth and elephant shrews urgently need to cool off!

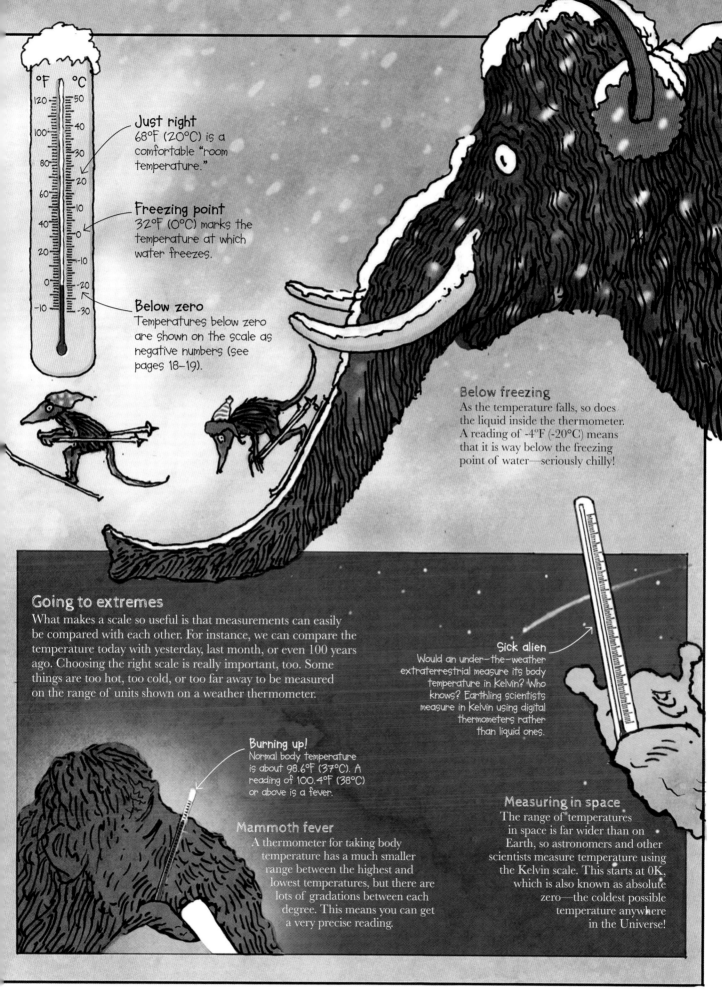

°F **°C**

Just right
68°F (20°C) is a
comfortable "room
temperature."

Freezing point
32°F (0°C) marks the
temperature at which
water freezes.

Below zero
Temperatures below zero
are shown on the scale as
negative numbers (see
pages 18–19).

Below freezing
As the temperature falls, so does
the liquid inside the thermometer.
A reading of -4°F (-20°C) means
that it is way below the freezing
point of water—seriously chilly!

Going to extremes

What makes a scale so useful is that measurements can easily
be compared with each other. For instance, we can compare the
temperature today with yesterday, last month, or even 100 years
ago. Choosing the right scale is really important, too. Some
things are too hot, too cold, or too far away to be measured
on the range of units shown on a weather thermometer.

Sick alien
Would an under-the-weather
extraterrestrial measure its body
temperature in Kelvin? Who
knows? Earthling scientists
measure in Kelvin using digital
thermometers rather
than liquid ones.

Burning up!
Normal body temperature
is about 98.6°F (37°C). A
reading of 100.4°F (38°C)
or above is a fever.

Mammoth fever
A thermometer for taking body
temperature has a much smaller
range between the highest and
lowest temperatures, but there are
lots of gradations between each
degree. This means you can get
a very precise reading.

Measuring in space
The range of temperatures
in space is far wider than on
Earth, so astronomers and other
scientists measure temperature using
the Kelvin scale. This starts at 0K,
which is also known as absolute
zero—the coldest possible
temperature anywhere
in the Universe!

Discovering data

Gathering data

"Data" is just another word for "information." Collecting, organizing, and trying to understand data is an area of mathematics called statistics. There are a number of different ways of collecting data. You could do a survey by asking a group of people questions and recording their answers. You could hold a vote. The mammoth is gathering data by observation, and using tally marks to make a record.

Days
Each day of the week has its own row in the tally chart.

Data sets
A collection of information about a subject is called a data set. Data sets can be split into smaller groups called subsets. In this data set of all the birds that visit, the subsets are the different bird species.

Tally marks
The mammoth makes a tally mark (see pages 10–11) for each bird that visits the table

Tracking bird behavior

The mammoth is using a frequency chart to collect information on which birds visit the feeding table. The chart lists the birds and the days of the week. The mammoths can then analyse the data they collect to work out how much bird food to stock up on. Also, by noting which birds visit less often, they might decide to put out a different food, to try to attract more.

Not a bird!
Furry paws suggest this strange species is an interloper.

Tempting treats
Five different bird species gather to eat at the feeder.

Types of data

Data in the form of numbers is called quantitative data. There are two main types: discrete and continuous. Discrete data is counted. It can only have certain values. For example, the number of children in a class is an example of discrete data, because you can't count half a child. Data that is measured is called continuous data. This kind of data can take any value in a range. It can also change over time.

Measuring height
Height is an example of continuous data because it can be any value within the range of possible human heights.

Counting goals
The total number of goals scored in a soccer tournament is an example of discrete data.

Data handling

Once you have collected your data, there are lots of ways to present it, to make it easier to analyze or understand. Drawing charts and graphs can make it easier to see the data clearly and to compare different subsets at a glance. Different types of charts are suited to showing different types of data.

What does it all mean?

The mammoth spent a whole week collecting data about the birds at a feeding table. To help explain the data to this avian audience, the mammoth has used it to draw three different charts.

Pie chart

These charts show subsets of data as slices of a circular "pie." They show how one part of a group compares to the whole amount. The mammoth has used a pie chart to show what proportion of the total number of birds across the week belonged to each species.

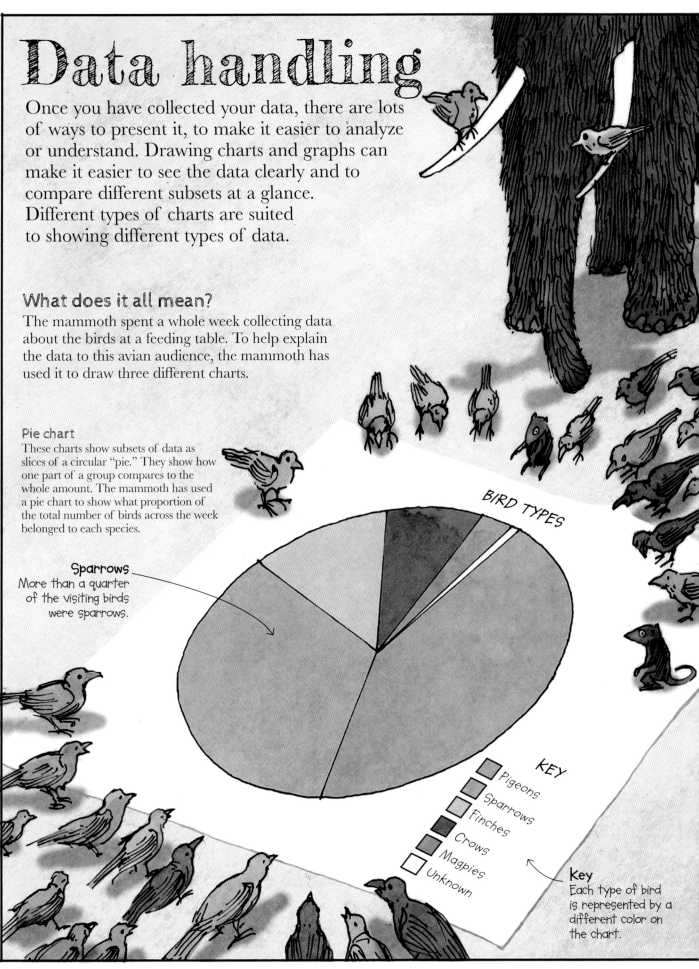

BIRD TYPES

Sparrows
More than a quarter of the visiting birds were sparrows.

KEY

- Pigeons
- Sparrows
- Finches
- Crows
- Magpies
- Unknown

Key
Each type of bird is represented by a different color on the chart.

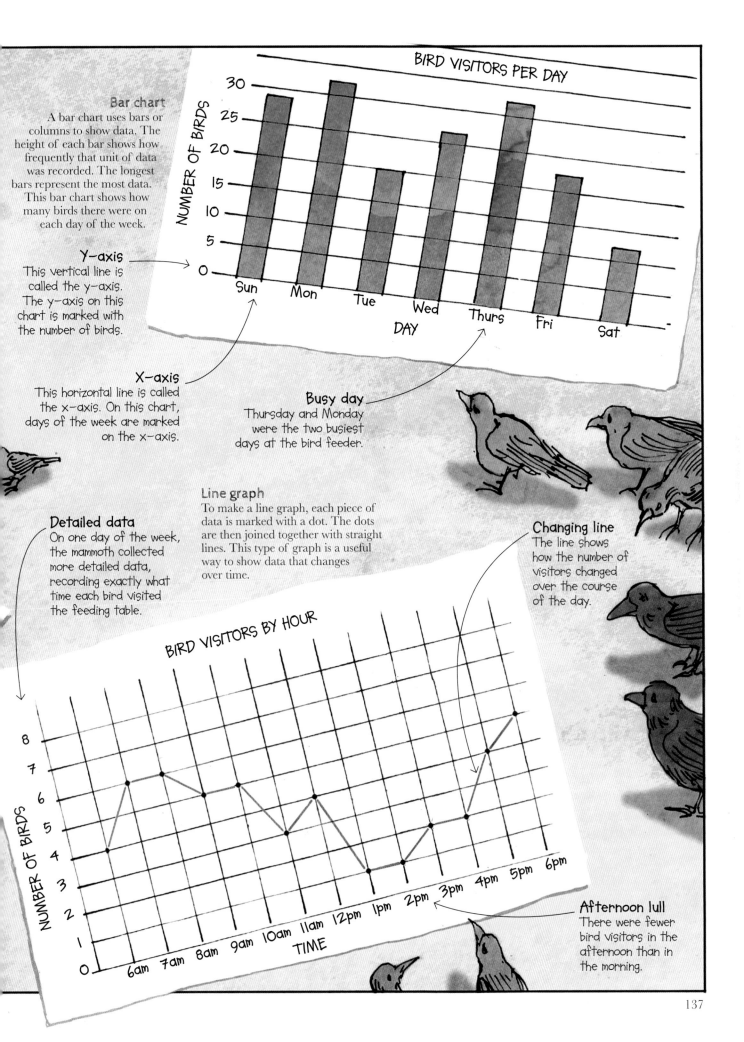

BIRD VISITORS PER DAY

Bar chart
A bar chart uses bars or columns to show data. The height of each bar shows how frequently that unit of data was recorded. The longest bars represent the most data. This bar chart shows how many birds there were on each day of the week.

Y-axis
This vertical line is called the y-axis. The y-axis on this chart is marked with the number of birds.

X-axis
This horizontal line is called the x-axis. On this chart, days of the week are marked on the x-axis.

Busy day
Thursday and Monday were the two busiest days at the bird feeder.

Detailed data
On one day of the week, the mammoth collected more detailed data, recording exactly what time each bird visited the feeding table.

Line graph
To make a line graph, each piece of data is marked with a dot. The dots are then joined together with straight lines. This type of graph is a useful way to show data that changes over time.

Changing line
The line shows how the number of visitors changed over the course of the day.

BIRD VISITORS BY HOUR

Afternoon lull
There were fewer bird visitors in the afternoon than in the morning.

Venn diagrams

If you have lots of things that fall into different groups, a Venn diagram could come in very handy. By organizing groups of things with similar characteristics (called sets) into overlapping circles, Venn diagrams show you which members of a group are similar and which are different.

Sets of sporty shrews

In math, a set is a group of things or numbers that have something in common. Whether they play soccer, have a hockey hobby, or love snorkelling, each of these elephant shrews belongs to a set. Those that enjoy more than one sport are in multiple sets—some are even in all three! To try and keep things under control, the mammoth has used a Venn diagram.

Soccer fanatics
Everyone in the orange circle likes playing soccer.

Soccer

The snorkelling soccer player
Because she likes both snorkelling and soccer, this shrew is in the space where the green and orange circles overlap.

Get set!

When the mammoth blows the whistle the shrews scramble to sort themselves into sets based on their favorite sports. Shrews who like every activity rush to the middle where all three circles in the Venn diagram overlap.

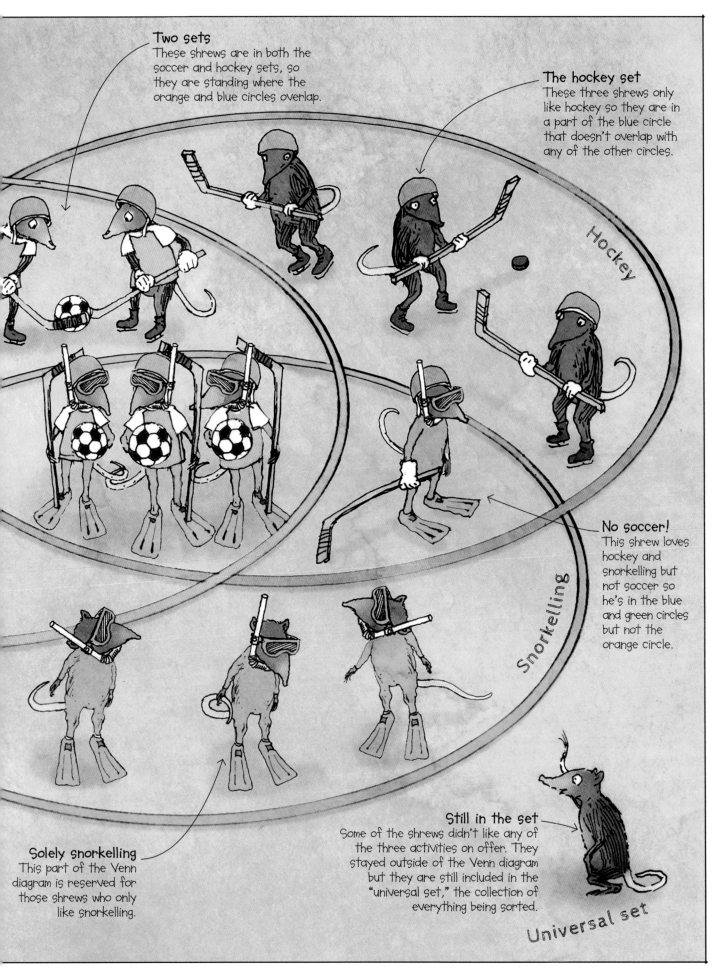

Two sets
These shrews are in both the soccer and hockey sets, so they are standing where the orange and blue circles overlap.

The hockey set
These three shrews only like hockey so they are in a part of the blue circle that doesn't overlap with any of the other circles.

Hockey

No soccer!
This shrew loves hockey and snorkelling but not soccer so he's in the blue and green circles but not the orange circle.

Snorkelling

Solely snorkelling
This part of the Venn diagram is reserved for those shrews who only like snorkelling.

Still in the set
Some of the shrews didn't like any of the three activities on offer. They stayed outside of the Venn diagram but they are still included in the "universal set," the collection of everything being sorted.

Universal set

Averages

An average is a type of middle value, which helps us summarize the data in a set. It's a way of representing the set by using a typical value to stand for the whole group. There are three different types of average: the mean, median, and mode.

Just an average day

This gang of mammoths are all different heights. The elephant shrews have measured each mammoth and then used that data to calculate the mean, the mode, and the median. They have used a bamboo pole to mark each different type of average.

5 m

4 m

3 m

2 m

1 m

Range
The difference between the largest and smallest values in the set is called the range. The biggest mammoth is 4 m and the smallest is 1.5 m, so the range of heights is 2.5 m.

4 m

Mode
This is the most common value in a set. Here the mode is 1.5 m as there are two mammoths who measure exactly that.

1.5 m

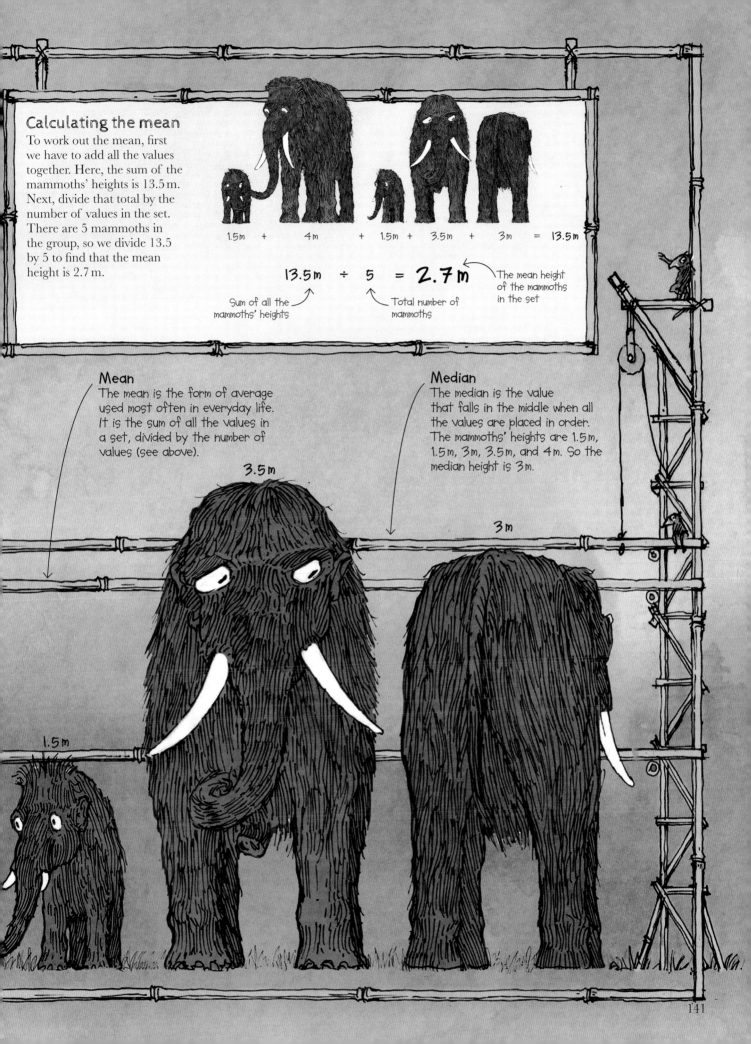

Calculating the mean

To work out the mean, first we have to add all the values together. Here, the sum of the mammoths' heights is 13.5 m. Next, divide that total by the number of values in the set. There are 5 mammoths in the group, so we divide 13.5 by 5 to find that the mean height is 2.7 m.

1.5 m + 4 m + 1.5 m + 3.5 m + 3 m = 13.5 m

$$13.5\,m \div 5 = 2.7\,m$$

Sum of all the mammoths' heights

Total number of mammoths

The mean height of the mammoths in the set

Mean

The mean is the form of average used most often in everyday life. It is the sum of all the values in a set, divided by the number of values (see above).

Median

The median is the value that falls in the middle when all the values are placed in order. The mammoths' heights are 1.5 m, 1.5 m, 3 m, 3.5 m, and 4 m. So the median height is 3 m.

3.5 m

3 m

1.5 m

Probability

The likelihood of something happening is called probability. An event with a higher probability is more likely to happen, while a lower probability means it is less likely. We often use fractions to describe probability. For example, a coin has two sides—heads and tails. When you flip it, the chance of it landing heads-up is 1 in 2, or $\frac{1}{2}$.

What are the chances?

This gargantuan chutes and ladders structure is a game of chance. The mammoths are taking turns to roll the die and see how many spaces their shrew partner will move on the board. On each roll of the die, there is a $\frac{1}{6}$ chance of rolling each of the six numbers on the die's faces. The purple-tusked mammoth is next to throw.

Good luck!

The purple shrew is in a perilous position. If its matching mammoth rolls a 1 or a 6, the shrew will land on a chute, while a 2 will send the shrew up the ladder. What are the shrew's chances of landing on a square that doesn't lead up a ladder or down a chute? (Answer on page 160.)

1-in-6

The die has six faces, but only one can land face-up.

Roll the die

If the mammoth rolls a 2, then the purple shrew is headed up the ladder, closer to victory. But rolling a 1 or a 6 will send the shrew tumbling down a chute. So the shrew has a $\frac{1}{6}$ chance of going up the ladder but the probability of going down a chute is greater, at $\frac{2}{6}$.

Wait your turn

These elephant shrews are lining up for a turn at the game.

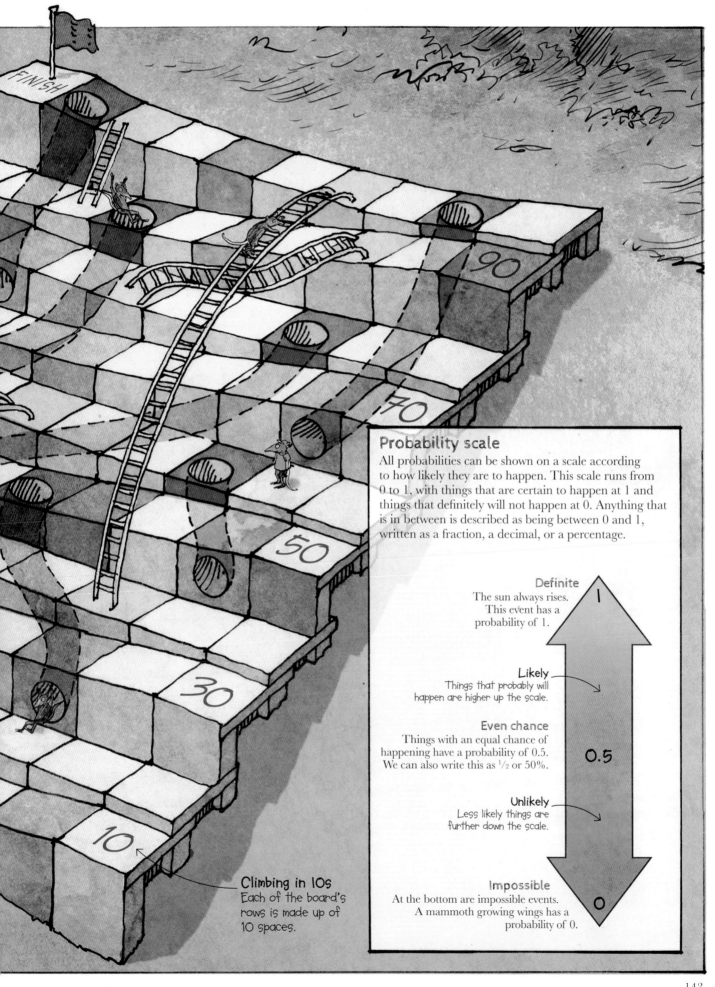

FINISH

90

70

Probability scale

All probabilities can be shown on a scale according to how likely they are to happen. This scale runs from 0 to 1, with things that are certain to happen at 1 and things that definitely will not happen at 0. Anything that is in between is described as being between 0 and 1, written as a fraction, a decimal, or a percentage.

50

30

Definite
The sun always rises.
This event has a
probability of 1.

1

Likely
Things that probably will
happen are higher up the scale.

Even chance
Things with an equal chance of
happening have a probability of 0.5.
We can also write this as $\frac{1}{2}$ or 50%.

0.5

Unlikely
Less likely things are
further down the scale.

10

Climbing in 10s
Each of the board's
rows is made up of
10 spaces.

Impossible
At the bottom are impossible events.
A mammoth growing wings has a
probability of 0.

0

Reference

Multiplication

Multiplication grid

You can use a grid like this to find the answers to multiplication calculations, or look up the answers in the tables on the opposite page.

$$6 \times 9 = 54$$

Second factor
Now find the second factor, 9, down the side of the grid.

X	1	2	3	4	5	6	7	8	9	10	11	12
1	1	2	3	4	5	6	7	8	9	10	11	12
2	2	4	6	8	10	12	14	16	18	20	22	24
3	3	6	9	12	15	18	21	24	27	30	33	36
4	4	8	12	16	20	24	28	32	36	40	44	48
5	5	10	15	20	25	30	35	40	45	50	55	60
6	6	12	18	24	30	36	42	48	54	60	66	72
7	7	14	21	28	35	42	49	56	63	70	77	84
8	8	16	24	32	40	48	56	64	72	80	88	96
9	9	18	27	36	45	54	63	72	81	90	99	108
10	10	20	30	40	50	60	70	80	90	100	110	120
11	11	22	33	44	55	66	77	88	99	110	121	132
12	12	24	36	48	60	72	84	96	108	120	132	144

Meeting point
The answer is 54—the number in the square where the two factors meet.

Squares grid

The multiplication grid also shows us square numbers up to 12. The square numbers make a diagonal line through the grid.

9 × 9 = 81
The point where the 9s meet on the grid is 81, which is the square of 9.

X	1	2	3	4	5	6	7	8	9	10	11	12
1	1	2	3	4	5	6	7	8	9	10	11	12
2	2	4	6	8	10	12	14	16	18	20	22	24
3	3	6	9	12	15	18	21	24	27	30	33	36
4	4	8	12	16	20	24	28	32	36	40	44	48
5	5	10	15	20	25	30	35	40	45	50	55	60
6	6	12	18	24	30	36	42	48	54	60	66	72
7	7	14	21	28	35	42	49	56	63	70	77	84
8	8	16	24	32	40	48	56	64	72	80	88	96
9	9	18	27	36	45	54	63	72	81	90	99	108
10	10	20	30	40	50	60	70	80	90	100	110	120
11	11	22	33	44	55	66	77	88	99	110	121	132
12	12	24	36	48	60	72	84	96	108	120	132	144

Multiplication tables

1 × table

1	×	1	=	1
1	×	2	=	2
1	×	3	=	3
1	×	4	=	4
1	×	5	=	5
1	×	6	=	6
1	×	7	=	7
1	×	8	=	8
1	×	9	=	9
1	×	10	=	10
1	×	11	=	11
1	×	12	=	12

2 × table

2	×	1	=	2
2	×	2	=	4
2	×	3	=	6
2	×	4	=	8
2	×	5	=	10
2	×	6	=	12
2	×	7	=	14
2	×	8	=	16
2	×	9	=	18
2	×	10	=	20
2	×	11	=	22
2	×	12	=	24

3 × table

3	×	1	=	3
3	×	2	=	6
3	×	3	=	9
3	×	4	=	12
3	×	5	=	15
3	×	6	=	18
3	×	7	=	21
3	×	8	=	24
3	×	9	=	27
3	×	10	=	30
3	×	11	=	33
3	×	12	=	36

4 × table

4	×	1	=	4
4	×	2	=	8
4	×	3	=	12
4	×	4	=	16
4	×	5	=	20
4	×	6	=	24
4	×	7	=	28
4	×	8	=	32
4	×	9	=	36
4	×	10	=	40
4	×	11	=	44
4	×	12	=	48

5 × table

5	×	1	=	5
5	×	2	=	10
5	×	3	=	15
5	×	4	=	20
5	×	5	=	25
5	×	6	=	30
5	×	7	=	35
5	×	8	=	40
5	×	9	=	45
5	×	10	=	50
5	×	11	=	55
5	×	12	=	60

6 × table

6	×	1	=	6
6	×	2	=	12
6	×	3	=	18
6	×	4	=	24
6	×	5	=	30
6	×	6	=	36
6	×	7	=	42
6	×	8	=	48
6	×	9	=	54
6	×	10	=	60
6	×	11	=	66
6	×	12	=	72

7 × table

7	×	1	=	7
7	×	2	=	14
7	×	3	=	21
7	×	4	=	28
7	×	5	=	35
7	×	6	=	42
7	×	7	=	49
7	×	8	=	56
7	×	9	=	63
7	×	10	=	70
7	×	11	=	77
7	×	12	=	84

8 × table

8	×	1	=	8
8	×	2	=	16
8	×	3	=	24
8	×	4	=	32
8	×	5	=	40
8	×	6	=	48
8	×	7	=	56
8	×	8	=	64
8	×	9	=	72
8	×	10	=	80
8	×	11	=	88
8	×	12	=	96

9 × table

9	×	1	=	9
9	×	2	=	18
9	×	3	=	27
9	×	4	=	36
9	×	5	=	45
9	×	6	=	54
9	×	7	=	63
9	×	8	=	72
9	×	9	=	81
9	×	10	=	90
9	×	11	=	99
9	×	12	=	108

10 × table

10	×	1	=	10
10	×	2	=	20
10	×	3	=	30
10	×	4	=	40
10	×	5	=	50
10	×	6	=	60
10	×	7	=	70
10	×	8	=	80
10	×	9	=	90
10	×	10	=	100
10	×	11	=	110
10	×	12	=	120

11 × table

11	×	1	=	11
11	×	2	=	22
11	×	3	=	33
11	×	4	=	44
11	×	5	=	55
11	×	6	=	66
11	×	7	=	77
11	×	8	=	88
11	×	9	=	99
11	×	10	=	110
11	×	11	=	121
11	×	12	=	132

12 × table

12	×	1	=	12
12	×	2	=	24
12	×	3	=	36
12	×	4	=	48
12	×	5	=	60
12	×	6	=	72
12	×	7	=	84
12	×	8	=	96
12	×	9	=	108
12	×	10	=	120
12	×	11	=	132
12	×	12	=	144

Fractions

The fraction wall

The wall shows which fractions are equivalent to each other—written differently but worth the same amount. For example, it shows that $^1/_2$, $^2/_4$, and $^4/_8$ are all equal.

1 Whole

$^1/_2$	$^1/_2$

$^1/_3$	$^1/_3$	$^1/_3$

$^1/_4$	$^1/_4$	$^1/_4$	$^1/_4$

$^1/_5$	$^1/_5$	$^1/_5$	$^1/_5$	$^1/_5$

$^1/_6$	$^1/_6$	$^1/_6$	$^1/_6$	$^1/_6$	$^1/_6$

$^1/_8$	$^1/_8$	$^1/_8$	$^1/_8$	$^1/_8$	$^1/_8$	$^1/_8$	$^1/_8$

$^1/_{10}$	$^1/_{10}$	$^1/_{10}$	$^1/_{10}$	$^1/_{10}$	$^1/_{10}$	$^1/_{10}$	$^1/_{10}$	$^1/_{10}$	$^1/_{10}$

$^1/_{12}$	$^1/_{12}$	$^1/_{12}$	$^1/_{12}$	$^1/_{12}$	$^1/_{12}$	$^1/_{12}$	$^1/_{12}$	$^1/_{12}$	$^1/_{12}$	$^1/_{12}$	$^1/_{12}$

Fractions, decimals, and percentages

There are many different ways you can show or write the same fraction. This table lists some of the most common fractions in all their different forms.

Part of a whole	Part of a group	Fraction in words	Fraction in numbers	Decimal	Percentage
		one-tenth	$^1/_{10}$	0.1	10%
		one-eighth	$^1/_8$	0.125	12.5%
		one-fifth	$^1/_5$	0.2	20%
		one-quarter	$^1/_4$	0.25	25%
		three-tenths	$^3/_{10}$	0.3	30%
		one-third	$^1/_3$	0.33	33%
		two-fifths	$^2/_5$	0.4	40%
		one-half	$^1/_2$	0.5	50%
		three-fifths	$^3/_5$	0.6	60%
		three-quarters	$^3/_4$	0.75	75%

Geometry

2D shapes

These polygons are named according to the Greek name for the number of sides and angles they have.

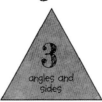
3 angles and sides
Equilateral triangle

3 angles and sides
Right-angled triangle

3 angles and sides
Isosceles triangle

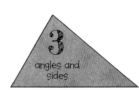
3 angles and sides
Scalene triangle

4 angles and sides
Square

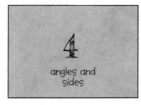
4 angles and sides
Rectangle

5 angles and sides
Pentagon

6 angles and sides
Hexagon

7 angles and sides
Heptagon

8 angles and sides
Octagon

9 angles and sides
Nonagon

10 angles and sides
Decagon

12 angles and sides
Dodecagon

20 angles and sides
Icosagon

3D shapes

3D shapes can be any shape or size. Here are some of the most common shapes in math.

Sphere

Cuboid

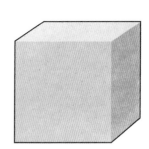
Cube

Triangular-based pyramid

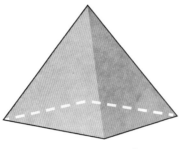
Square-based pyramid

Cone

Cylinder

Parts of a circle

A circle has parts that no other shape has.
Here are some of the most important parts.

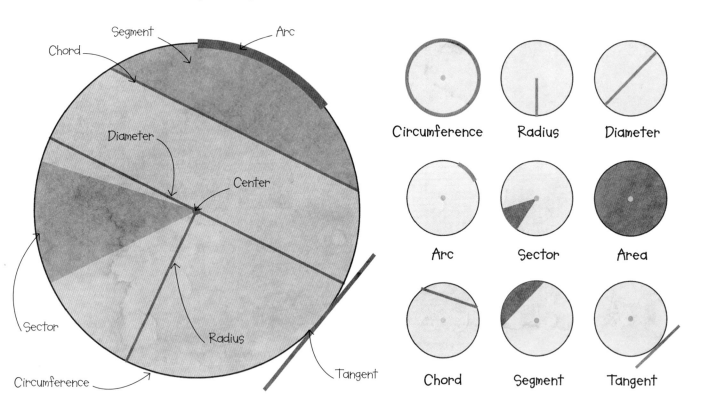

Angles

Angles have names according to their size.
There are five types of angle.

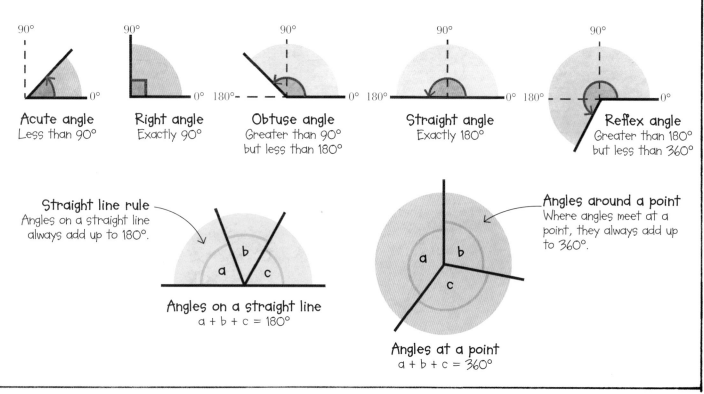

Acute angle
Less than 90°

Right angle
Exactly 90°

Obtuse angle
Greater than 90°
but less than 180°

Straight angle
Exactly 180°

Reflex angle
Greater than 180°
but less than 360°

Straight line rule
Angles on a straight line
always add up to 180°.

Angles on a straight line
a + b + c = 180°

Angles around a point
Where angles meet at a
point, they always add up
to 360°.

Angles at a point
a + b + c = 360°

Units of measurement

Units of measurement
Using standard units of measurement helps us compare things accurately. There are two common systems of measurement: the metric system and the imperial system.

LENGTH

Metric

10 millimeters (mm)	=	1 centimeter (cm)
100 centimeters (cm)	=	1 meter (m)
1,000 millimeters (mm)	=	1 meter (m)
1,000 meters (m)	=	1 kilometer (km)

Imperial

12 inches (in)	=	1 foot (ft)
3 feet (ft)	=	1 yard (yd)
1,760 yards (yd)	=	1 mile
5,280 feet (ft)	=	1 mile
8 furlongs	=	1 mile

AREA

Metric

100 square millimeters (mm²)	=	1 square centimeter (cm²)
10,000 square centimeters (cm²)	=	1 square meter (m²)
10,000 square meters (m²)	=	1 hectare (ha)
100 hectares (ha)	=	1 square kilometer (km²)
1 square kilometer (km²)	=	1,000,000 sq meters (m²)

Imperial

144 square inches (sq in)	=	1 square foot (sq ft)
9 square feet (sq ft)	=	1 square yard (sq yd)
1,296 square inches (sq in)	=	1 square yard (sq yd)
43,560 square feet (sq ft)	=	1 acre
640 acres	=	1 square mile (sq mile)

MASS

Metric

1,000 milligrams (mg)	=	1 gram (g)
1,000 grams (g)	=	1 kilogram (kg)
1,000 kilograms (kg)	=	1 metric ton (t)

Imperial

16 ounces (oz)	=	1 pound (lb)
14 pounds (lb)	=	1 stone (st)
112 pounds (lb)	=	1 hundredweight (cwt)
20 hundredweight (cwt)	=	1 ton

TIME

Metric and Imperial

60 seconds	=	1 minute
60 minutes	=	1 hour
24 hours	=	1 day
7 days	=	1 week
52 weeks	=	1 year
1 year	=	12 months

TEMPERATURE

		Fahrenheit	Celsius	Kelvin
Boiling point of water	=	212°	100°	373
Freezing point of water	=	32°	0°	273
Absolute zero	=	-459°	-273°	0

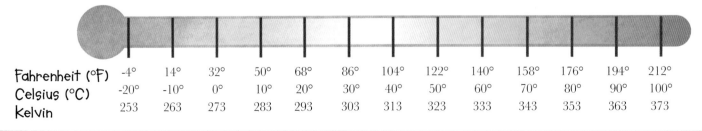

Fahrenheit (°F)	-4°	14°	32°	50°	68°	86°	104°	122°	140°	158°	176°	194°	212°
Celsius (°C)	-20°	-10°	0°	10°	20°	30°	40°	50°	60°	70°	80°	90°	100°
Kelvin	253	263	273	283	293	303	313	323	333	343	353	363	373

Conversion tables

The tables below give the metric and imperial equivalents for some common measurements.

LENGTH

Metric		Imperial
1 millimeter (mm)	=	0.03937 inch (in)
1 centimeter (cm)	=	0.3937 inch (in)
1 meter (m)	=	1.0936 yards (yd)
1 kilometer (km)	=	0.6214 mile

Imperial		Metric
1 inch (in)	=	2.54 centimeters (cm)
1 foot (ft)	=	0.3048 meter (m)
1 yard (yd)	=	0.9144 meter (m)
1 mile	=	1.6093 kilometers (km)
1 nautical mile	=	1.853 kilometers (km)

AREA

Metric		Imperial
1 square centimeter (cm^2)	=	0.155 square inch (sq in)
1 square meter (m^2)	=	1.196 square yards (sq yd)
1 hectare (ha)	=	2.4711 acres
1 square kilometer (km^2)	=	0.3861 square miles

Imperial		Metric
1 square inch (sq in)	=	6.4516 square centimeters (cm^2)
1 square foot (sq ft)	=	0.0929 square meter (m^2)
1 square yard (sq yd)	=	0.8361 square meter (m^2)
1 acre	=	0.4047 hectare (ha)
1 square mile	=	2.59 square kilometers (km^2)

MASS

Metric		Imperial
1 milligram (mg)	=	0.0154 grain
1 gram (g)	=	0.0353 ounce (oz)
1 kilogram (kg)	=	2.2046 pounds (lb)
1 tonne/metric ton (t)	=	0.9842 ton/imperial ton

Imperial		Metric
1 ounce (oz)	=	28.35 grams (g)
1 pound (lb)	=	0.4536 kilograms (kg)
1 stone	=	6.3503 kilograms (kg)
1 hundredweight (cwt)	=	50.802 kilograms (kg)
1 ton/imperial ton	=	1.016 tonnes/metric tons (t)

Signs and symbols

There are lots of symbols used in math to represent different operations or values. Here are some of the most common.

$=$	is equal to
$<$	is less than
$>$	is greater than
$\approx$	is approximately equal to
$+$	add, plus
$-$	subtract, take away
$\times$	multiply by, times
$\div$	divide by
$\sqrt{}$	square root
$\%$	percent
π	Pi
∞	infinity

Glossary

ALGEBRA
Using symbols such as letters to stand for unknown numbers in calculations.

ANGLE
The amount of turn between two lines that meet at a vertex (corner). Angles are measured in *degrees*.

ARC
A curved line that forms part of the circumference of a circle.

AREA
The amount of space inside a 2D shape. We measure area in square units, such as square meters.

ARRAY
An arrangement of objects or numbers in a pattern that has equal rows and columns.

AVERAGE
The typical or middle value of a group of numbers or set of data. The three different kinds of average are the *mean*, *median*, and *mode*.

COORDINATES
A coordinate is a pair of numbers that describes the position of a point on a graph, grid, or map.

CROSS SECTION
When you cut through a prism parallel to one of its ends, the new face you make is a called a cross section.

CUBED NUMBER
The result of multiplying a number by itself twice. 27 is a cubed number, because 3 x 3 x 3 = 27.

DATA
Information or facts that we collect so they can be analyzed, such as a set of measurements.

DECIMAL POINT
The dot that separates a whole number from the fraction part, as in the number 4.5.

DECIMAL SYSTEM
The number system we use, based on the number 10, and which uses the digits 0, 1, 2, 3, 4, 5, 6, 7, 8, and 9.

DEGREE
We measure angles in units called degrees, using this symbol: °.

DENOMINATOR
The number under the dividing line in a fraction, such as the 2 in ¹/₂.

DIGIT
The symbols we use to write numbers. The ten digits in our number system are 0, 1, 2, 3, 4, 5, 6, 7, 8, and 9.

ELEPHANT SHREW
A small, rodent-like mammal with a long snout. Also known as a sengi.

EQUATION
A statement that says something is equal to something else. An example is 6 + 2 = 10 - 2.

FACTOR
A number that divides exactly into another number. For example, 3 is a factor of 9.

FAHRENHEIT
A scale of temperature, named after Gabriel Fahrenheit, a scientist who invented the mercury thermometer in 1714.

FIBONACCI
As well as producing his smart number sequence, Leonardo Fibonacci was the first European to use the *Hindu-Arabic* number system that we still use today.

FORMULA
A rule that describes the link between things, usually written with symbols instead of numbers.

FRACTION
A part of a whole number or an amount. The same fraction can be written in different ways, such as ¹/₂, 50%, or 0.5.

GEOMETRY
The branch of math that studies shapes, lines, angles, and spaces.

GRID
Horizontal and vertical lines that criss-cross to make a network of equal-size squares.

HINDU-ARABIC
The name for our number system, which uses the digits 0–9. It was originally invented by Indian scientists more than 2,000 years ago.

IMPERIAL SYSTEM
Traditional ways of measuring, such as feet and inches, and gallons and pints. Scientists and mathematicians now use the *metric system* instead.

IMPROPER FRACTION
A fraction, such as ⁵/₂, that is greater than 1. The *numerator* is larger than the *denominator*.

INTERSECT
When lines meet or shapes cross over each other, they intersect.

KELVIN
A scale of temperature invented by Lord Kelvin, a British scientist who also explained how heat moves through substances.

LINE OF SYMMETRY
A line you can draw through a 2D shape that acts like a mirror, dividing it into identical halves.

MEAN
An *average* that you find by adding up all the values in a data set, then dividing the total by the number of values.

MEDIAN
An *average* that's the middle value of a set of data, when the values are put in order from highest to lowest.

METRIC SYSTEM
A way of measuring things such as length or weight, that is based on units of 10. This makes calculations much easier!

MIXED NUMBER
A number that is made up of a whole number and a fraction, such as 3¹/₂.

MODE
An *average* that is the value that appears most often in a set of data.

MULTIPLE
The number that you get when you multiply two numbers together. 8 is a multiple of 4, and also of 2.

NEGATIVE NUMBER
A number that is less than zero, such as -2. Decimal numbers can be negative, too.

NET
A flat shape that can be folded to make a 3D object.

NON-UNIT FRACTION
A fraction that has a *numerator* greater than 1, such as $^4/_5$.

NUMBER LINE
A line marked with evenly spaced whole numbers, fractions, or decimals. Number lines are used for counting and calculations.

NUMERATOR
The number above the dividing line in a fraction, such as the 1 in $^1/_2$.

OPERATION
An action that you can do on a number, such as addition, subtraction, division, or multiplication.

PASCAL
French genius Blaise Pascal made many important math and science discoveries. In 1661, he even launched the world's first bus service!

PERCENTAGE
A kind of fraction that uses the symbol % to show that it is a fraction of 100. The percentage 30% is the same as $^{30}/_{100}$.

PERIMETER
The distance all the way around the edges of a shape.

PERPENDICULAR
When a line is at right angles to another, it is perpendicular.

PIE CHART
A diagram that shows data as sectors of a circle, which look like slices of a pie.

PLACE-VALUE SYSTEM
Our way of writing numbers, where the value of each digit depends on its place in a number. The 3 in 130 has a value of thirty, but in 310, its value is three hundred.

POSITIVE NUMBER
A number that is more than zero, such as 25. Fractions and decimals can be positive, too.

PROBABILITY
The measurement of how likely something is to happen.

PROPER FRACTION
A fraction where the *numerator* is smaller than the *denominator*. $^2/_3$ is a proper fraction.

PROPORTION
A way of using fractions to compare the size of something that is part of a whole to the whole thing. The number 1 is $^1/_4$ the size of the number 4.

PROTRACTOR
A tool that helps us draw or measure angles.

PYTHAGORAS
An ancient Greek thinker. As well as coming up with his triangles theorem, he was one of the first people to work out that Earth is round.

QUOTIENT
The answer you get when you divide one number by another.

RADIUS
Any straight line from the center of a circle to its circumference. The plural is "radii."

RANGE
The spread of values in a set of data, from the lowest to the highest.

RATIO
A way of comparing one number or amount with another. It is written as two numbers, separated by a colon (:).

ROUNDING
Changing one number to a another that is close to it in value but is easier to work with. For example, you can round 2.1 to 2, or 1,950 to 2,000.

SEQUENCE
A set of numbers or shapes that follow a particular rule.

SET
A collection of things that have something in common, such as words, numbers, or shapes.

SIGNIFICANT DIGITS
The digits of a number that affect its value the most.

SIMPLIFY
To put something, such as a fraction, into its simplest form to make it easier to work with. For example, you can simplify $^6/_9$ to $^2/_3$.

SQUARED NUMBER
The result of multiplying a number by itself. 25 is a square number, because $5 \times 5 = 25$.

SUBSET
A *set* that is part of a larger set.

THREE-DIMENSIONAL (3D)
Having length, width, and depth. All solid objects, like spheres or cubes, are three-dimensional.

TRANSFORMATION
Changing the size or position of a shape or object. The three types of transformation are reflection, rotation, and translation.

TURN
To move round a fixed point, such as the movement of the hands of a clock.

TWO-DIMENSIONAL (2D)
Having length and width or length and height, but no thickness. All polygons, like triangles, are two-dimensional.

UNIT
A standard size that we use for measuring things. A meter is a unit of length and a gram is a unit of mass.

UNIT FRACTION
A fraction in which the *numerator* is 1, such as $^1/_5$.

UNIVERSAL SET
The largest *set*, which includes all the data and subsets in a collection.

VALUE
The amount or size of a number or object.

VARIABLE
An unknown number or amount. In algebra, a variable is usually shown as a letter or a symbol.

VERTEX
An angled corner of a 2D or 3D shape. The plural is "vertices."

VOLUME
The three-dimensional size of an object. It's measured in units cubed, such as cubic meters (m^3).

WHOLE NUMBER
A number that is not a fraction. 0, 15, and 235 are all whole numbers.

X-AXIS
The horizontal line that we use to measure the position of points on a map, grid, or graph.

Y-AXIS
The vertical line that we use to measure the position of points on a map, grid, or graph.

Index

Solutions

p.53
¾ of the dye in the pool is red.

p.58
The next 5 terms in the mammoth's shirt sequence are 12, 14, 16, 18, and 20.

The next term in the elephant shrew's shirt sequence is 2 (the rule is "subtract 3 to find the next term").

p.62
There will be 25 blue squares when the mammoth has finished stamping 5².

p.68

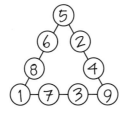

p.70
The totals of the horizontal rows are all powers of 2:
1 x 2 = 2, 2 x 2 = 4, 2 x 4 = 8, 2 x 16 = 32, 2 x 32 = 64.

p.90

p.109
There are 34 irregular shapes in the mammoth model.

p.111
There are 11 nets of a cube:

p.142
The chances of the purple elephant shrew landing on a square that doesn't lead up a ladder or down a chute are ³/₆, which is the same as ¹/₂.